CROCHET VARIETY

gifts and bric-a-brac

Nanette Esterhuyse
(compiler)

δελος

Delos 40 Heerengracht Cape Town

Set in 10 on 11 pt Helvetica Roman
Printed and bound by National Book Printers,
Goodwood, Cape
First edition, first impression 1989
Second impression 1989

ISBN 1 86826 008 9

General Information

CROCHET ABBREVIATIONS:

ch	– chain
ss	– slip stitch
dc	– double crochet
half tr	– half treble
tr	– treble
dbl tr	– double treble
trip tr	– triple treble
quad tr	– quadruple treble
lp(s)	– loop(s)
sp(s)	– space(s)
st	– stitch(es)
cl(s)	– cluster(s)
pc st(s)	– popcorn st(es)
p	– picot
inc(s)	– increase(s)
cont	– continue
beg	– beginning
rep	– repeat
M	– main colour
C	– contrasting colour
blk(s)	– block(s) = 4 tr plus 3 tr for each additional block in group
sp(s)	– space(s) = 2 ch, miss 2 ch or tr, 1 tr into next ch or tr (filet crochet)

***ASTERISK:** Repeat instructions following the asterisk as many more times as specified in addition to the original. For example * 1 tr into next tr, 3ch; repeat from * 3 times more, means that there are 4 patterns in all.

PARENTHESIS: Repeat instructions in parenthesis as many times as specified. For example, "(3ch, 1dc into next sp) 5 times", means to make all that is in parenthesis 5 times in all.

It is advisable to purchase at one time the number of balls sufficient for your requirements.

TENSION: Check this carefully before commencing your design as only the correct tension will ensure the best finished specimens. If your work is loose use a size finer hook/needle, if tight use a size larger hook/needle.

LAUNDERING CROCHET: Mercer-Crochet colours are fast dyed and are highly resistant to even the most severe washing treatments but these colours may be adversely affected when washed in certain commercial washing preparations which contain high levels of fluorescent brightening (whitening) agents. To maintain the true tones of Mercer-Crochet colours it is recommended that pure soap flakes type washing agents be used as these generally contain only low concentrations of fluorescent brightening (whitening) agents. Items should not be washed when work is still in progress. The assembled article should be washed on completion.

Make a warm lather of pure soap flakes and wash in the usual way, either by hand or washing machine. If desired, the article may be spin dried until it is damp, or left until it is half dry.

FASHIONING: Place a piece of paper, either plain white or squared, on top of a clean, flat board. Following the correct measurements, draw the shape of the finished article on to the paper, using ruler and set square for squares and rectangles and a pair of compasses for circles. Using rustless pins, pin the article out to the pencilled shape, taking care not to train the work. Pin out the general shape first, then finish by pinning each picot, loop or space into position. Special points to note carefully when pinning out are:

1. When pinning loops, make sure the pin is in the centre of each loop to form balanced lines.
2. When pinning scallops, make all the scallops the same size and regularly curved.
3. Pull out all picots.
4. Where there are flowers, pull out each petal in position.
5. When pinning filet crochet, make sure that the spaces and blocks are square and that all edges are even and straight.

If the work requires to be slightly stiffened, use a solution of starch – 1 dessertspoonful to $\frac{1}{2}$ litre (1 pint) hot water, and dab lightly over the article. Raise the work up off the paper, to prevent it sticking as it dries. When dry, remove the pins and press the article lightly with a hot iron.

Easter Bunny Egg Cosies

MATERIALS: Coats Chain Mercer-Crochet Cotton No. 20: 20 g Brown (M), 20 g White (M), 10 g each of Pink (C) and Yellow. Small length of Shaded Green. Milward steel crochet hook 1,25 mm. 30 cm Berisford Ribbon, 3 mm wide for each rabbit. Cotton wool for stuffing heads and tails.

The above quantities are sufficient for 2 brown rabbits and 2 white rabbits.

TENSION: First 4 rows – 2,5 cm in diameter.

FINISHED SIZE: 11 cm high approximately.

ABBREVIATIONS: See p. 3

BODY: Using M commence with 2 ch.
1st Row: 6 dc into 2nd ch from hook, 1 ss into first dc.
2nd Row: 3 ch, 2 tr into same place as ss, 3 tr into each dc, 1 ss into 3rd of 3 ch.
3rd Row: 1 dc into same place as ss, 1 dc into each tr, 1 ss into first dc.
4th Row: 3 ch, 1 tr into same place as ss, 2 tr into each dc, 1 ss into 3rd of 3 ch.
5th Row: As 3rd row.
6th Row: 3 ch, 1 tr into same place as ss, * 1 tr into next dc, 2 tr into next dc; rep from * ending with 1 tr into next dc, 1 ss into 3rd of 3 ch.
7th Row: As 3rd row.
8th Row: 3 ch, 1 tr into same place as ss, * 1 tr into each of next 2 dc, 2 tr into next dc; rep from * omitting 2 tr at end of last rep, 1 ss into 3rd of 3 ch.
9th Row: As 3rd row.
10th Row: 3 ch, 1 tr into each dc, 1 ss into 3rd of 3 ch.
Rep 9th and 10th rows 5 times more then 9th row again. Fasten off.

HEAD: Using M commence with 2 ch.
1st Row: 6 dc into 2nd ch from hook.
2nd Row: 2 dc into each dc. (12 dc).
3rd Row: 2 dc into each dc. (24 dc).
4th Row: 1 dc into each dc.
5th Row: (2 dc into next dc, 1 dc into next dc) 12 times. (36 dc).
6th and 7th Rows: As 4th row.
8th Row: (2 dc into next dc, 1 dc into each of next 5 dc) 6 times. (42 dc).
9th Row: As 4th row.
10th Row: (2 dc into next dc, 1 dc into each of next 6 dc) 6 times. (48 dc).
11th to 17th Row: As 4th row.
18th Row: * (Insert hook into next dc and draw thread through) twice, thread over and draw through all lps on hook (a joint dc made), 1 dc into each of next 6 dc; rep from * 5 times more. (42 sts).
19th to 20th Rows: As 4th row.
21st Row: (A joint dc over next 2 dc, 1 dc into each of next 5 dc) 6 times. (36 sts).
22nd and 23rd Rows: As 4th row. Fasten off.

EAR (make 2): Using C commence with 6 ch, join with a ss to form a ring.
1st Row: 8 dc into ring, 1 ch, turn.
2nd to 11th Row: 1 dc into each dc, 1 ch, turn.
12th Row: 1 dc into each of first 3 dc, a joint dc over next 2 dc, 1 dc into each dc, 1 ch, turn.
13th Row: 1 dc into each st, 1 ch, turn.
14th Row: A joint dc over first 2 dc, 1 dc into each of next 3 dc, a joint dc over next 2 dc, 1 ch, turn.
15th Row: As 13th row.
16th Row: A joint dc over first 2 dc, 1 dc into next dc, a joint dc over next 2 dc, 1 ch, turn.
17th Row: As 13th row.
18th Row: Insert hook into first dc and draw thread through, (insert hook into next dc and draw thread through) twice, thread over and draw through all lps on hook, 1 ch, turn.
19th Row: 1 dc into st. Fasten off.

EDGING: With right side facing attach M to first row end, 1 dc into same place as join, 1 dc over each of next 17 row ends, 1 ch, 5 tr into dc on 19th row, 1 ch, 1 dc over each of next 18 row ends, 1 ss into first dc. Fasten off.

EYE (make 2): Using C commence with 2 ch.
1st Row: 6 dc into 2nd ch from hook, 1 ss into first dc. Fasten off.
2nd Row: Attach M (white for brown rabbit or brown for white rabbit) to same place as ss, 1 dc into same place as join, 2 hlf tr into next dc, 3 tr into next dc, 2 hlf tr into next dc, 1 dc into next dc, 1 ss into next dc, 1 ss into first dc. Fasten off.

TAIL: Using C work as Head for 2 rows.
3rd Row: (2 dc into next dc, 1 dc into next dc) 6 times. (18 dc).
4th to 6th Row: 1 dc into each dc.
7th Row: (A joint dc over next 2 dc, 1 dc into each of next 2 dc) 6 times. (12 dc).
8th Row: 1 dc into each dc. Fasten off leaving sufficient to thread through last row. Stuff with cotton wool and draw up last row.

CARROT: Using Yellow commence with 4 ch.
1st Row: 7 tr into 4th ch from hook, 1 ss into 4th of 4 ch.
2nd Row: 1 dc into same place as ss, 1 dc into each tr, 1 ss into first dc.
3rd Row: 3 ch, 1 tr into same place as ss, (1 tr into next dc, 2 tr into next dc) 3 times, 1 tr into next dc, 1 ss into 3rd of 3 ch.
4th Row: As 2nd row.
5th Row: 3 ch, 1 tr into same place as ss, (1 tr into each of next 2 dc, 2 tr into next dc) 3 times, 1 tr into each of next 2 dc, 1 ss into 3rd of 3 ch.
6th Row: As 2nd row.
7th Row: 3 ch, 1 tr into same place as ss, (1 tr into each of next 3 dc, 2 tr into next dc) 3 times, 1 tr into each of next 3 dc, 1 ss into 3rd of 3 ch.
8th Row: As 2nd row.
9th Row: 3 ch, 1 tr into each dc, 1 ss into 3rd of 3 ch.
10th Row: 1 dc into same place as ss, 1 dc into each tr, 1 ss into back lp of first dc.
11th Row: 2 ch, work into back lp only of each dc, 1 tr into next dc, leaving

the last lp of each on hook work 1 tr into each of next 2 dc, thread over and draw through all lps on hook (a joint tr made), (a joint tr over next 2 dc) 8 times, 1 ss into first tr. Fasten off leaving sufficient to thread through last row. Stuff with cotton wool and draw up last row.

LEAVES: Using Green commence with 8 ch.

1st Row: * (1 dc into 8th ch from hook, 8 ch) twice, 1 dc into 8th ch from hook, 9 ch, 1 dc into 9th ch from hook, 10 ch, 1 dc into 10th ch from hook, 11 ch, into same place as last dc work 1 dc 10 ch and 1 dc, 9 ch, 1 dc over next dc, (8 ch, 1 dc over next dc) 3 times, 8 ch; rep from * once more omitting 8 ch at end of rep. Fasten off.

Damp and starch then pull all pieces into shape.

TO MAKE UP: Stuff head then sew eyes and ears in position. Using contrasting colours apply whiskers and teeth as shown in illustration. Sew head to body and leaves to carrot. Tie ribbon neatly in a bow at neck then sew carrot and tail in position.

Milk Jug Cover

MATERIALS: Coats Chain Mercer-Crochet Cotton No. 20 (20 g): 1 ball selected colour, 1 ball contrasting colour. Milward steel crochet hook 1,25 mm, 24 small beads.

TENSION: First row – 2,5 cm in diameter.

MEASUREMENT: Finished size – 18 cm in diameter.

ABBREVIATIONS: See p. 3

Before commencing thread beads on to ball of M. Using M commence with 12 ch, join with a ss to form a ring.

1st Row: 3 ch, leaving the last lp of each on hook work 3 dbl tr into ring, thread over and draw through all lps on hook (a 3 dbl tr cl made), (6 ch, a 4 dbl tr cl into ring) 7 times, 6 ch, 1 ss into first cl.

2nd Row: Into each lp work 1 dc 1 hlf tr 6 tr 1 hlf tr and 1 dc, 1 ss into back lp of first dc.

3rd Row: * 7 ch, inserting hook from behind work 1 dc into next cl on 1st row; repeat from * ending with 7 ch.

4th Row: Into each lp work 1 dc 1 hlf tr 7 tr 1 hlf tr and 1 dc, 1 ss into back lp of first dc.

5th Row: * 8 ch, inserting hook from behind work 1 dc into next dc on 3rd row; rep from * ending with 8 ch.

6th Row: Into each lp word 1 dc 1 hlf tr 8 tr 1 hlf tr and 1 dc, 1 ss into back lp of first dc.

7th Row: * 9 ch, inserting hook from behind work 1 dc into next dc on 5th row; rep from * ending with 9 ch.

8th Row: Into each lp word 1 dc 1 hlf tr 9 tr 1 hlf tr and 1 dc, 1 ss into back lp of first dc.

9th Row: 1 dc into same place as ss, * 5 ch, 1 tr into last dc (5 ch, 1 tr into top of last tr) twice, inserting hook from behind work 1 dc into next dc on 7th row; rep from * omitting 1 dc at end of last rep, 1 ss into first dc.

10th Row: 1 ss into next ch, into same lp work 1 dc 3 ch and 1 dc, * 5 ch, into next lp work 1 dc 3 ch and 1 dc; rep from * ending with 2 ch, 1 tr into first dc.

11th to 14th Row: Into lp just formed work 1 dc 3 ch and 1 dc, * 5 ch, into next 5 ch lp work 1 dc 3 ch and 1 dc; rep from * ending with 2 ch, 1 tr into first dc.

15th Row: Into lp just formed work 1 dc 3 ch and 1 dc, * 6 ch, into next 5 ch lp work 1 dc 3 ch and 1 dc; rep from * ending with 2 ch, 1 dbl tr into first dc.

16th Row: Into lp just formed work 1 dc 3 ch and 1 dc, * 7 ch, into next 6 ch lp work 1 dc 3 ch and 1 dc; rep from * ending with 3 ch, 1 dbl tr into first dc.

17th Row: Into lp just formed work 1 dc 3 ch and 1 dc, * 8 ch, into next 7 ch lp work 1 dc 3 ch and 1 dc; rep from * ending with 3 ch, 1 trip tr into first dc.

18th and 19th Row: Into lp just formed work 1 dc 3 and 1 dc, * 9 ch, into next 8 ch lp work 1 dc 3 ch and 1 dc; rep from * ending with 4 ch, 1 trip tr into first dc.

20th Row: Into lp just formed work 1 dc 3 ch and 1 dc, * 5 ch, draw up 1 bead and secure with 1 ch, 5 ch, into next 9 ch lp work 1 dc 3 ch and 1 dc; rep from * omitting 1 dc 3 ch and 1 dc at end of last rep, 1 ss into first dc. Fasten off.

LEAF (make 8): Using C commence with 8 ch.

1st Row: 1 dc into 2nd ch from hook, 1 dc into each ch, 1 ch, turn.

2nd Row: 1 dc into first dc, 1 hlf tr into next dc, 2 tr into next dc, 3 tr into next dc, 2 tr into next dc, 1 hlf tr into next dc, 3 dc into next dc, working over 1st row work 1 hlf tr into same place as last hlf tr, 2 tr into same place as next 2 tr, 3 tr into same place as next 3 tr, 2 tr into same place as next 2 tr, 1 hlf tr into same place as next hlf tr, 1 dc into same place as next dc, 1 ch, turn.

3rd Row: 1 dc into each of first 11 sts, into next dc work 1 dc 2 ch and 1 dc, 1 dc into each st, 1 ss into first dc. Fasten off.

Damp and pin out to measurement. Sew leaves in position as shown in illustration.

Pot holder

MATERIALS: Tridalia No. 8: 20 g main colour, 10 g contrasting colour. Milward steel crochet hook 1,50 mm. The above quantity is sufficient for one pot holder.

TENSION: First 4 rows – 4 cm in diameter.

MEASUREMENTS: 24 cm from point to point.

ABBREVIATIONS: See p. 3

Using M commence with 12 ch, join with a ss to form a ring.
1st Row: 24 dc into ring, 1 ss into first dc.
2nd Row: 1 dc into same place as ss, * 3 ch, miss 1 dc, 1 dc into next dc; rep from * ending with 3 ch, 1 ss into first dc.
3rd Row: 1 ss into next lp, 3 ch, into same lp work 2 tr 1 ch and 3 tr, * miss next lp, into next lp work 3 tr 1 ch and 3 tr; rep from * ending with 1 ss into 3rd of 3 ch.
4th Row: 3 ch, 1 tr into next tr, * 2 tr into next tr, 3 ch, 2 tr into next tr, 1 tr into each of next 4 tr; rep from * omitting 2 tr at end of last rep, 1 ss into 3rd of 3 ch.
5th Row: 3 ch, 1 tr into each of next 2 tr, * 2 tr into next tr, into next sp work 1 tr 3 ch and 1 tr (a V st made), 2 tr into next tr, 1 tr into each of next 6 tr; rep from * omitting 3 tr at end of last rep, 1 ss into 3rd of 3 ch.
6th Row: 3 ch, 1 tr into each of next 4 tr, * 2 tr into next tr, 3 ch, 2 tr into next tr, 1 tr into each of next 10 tr; rep from * omitting 5 tr at end of last rep, 1 ss into 3rd of 3 ch.
7th Row: 3 ch, 1 tr into each of next 5 tr, * 2 tr into next tr, a V st into next sp, 2 tr into next tr, 1 tr into each of next 12 tr; rep from * omitting 6 tr at end of last rep, 1 ss into 3rd of 3 ch.
8th Row: 3 ch, 1 tr into each of next 7 tr, * 2 tr into next tr, 3 ch, 2 tr into next tr, 1 tr into each of next 16 tr; rep from * omitting 8 tr at end of last rep, 1 ss into 3rd of 3 ch.
9th Row: 3 ch, 1 tr into each of next 8 tr, * 2 tr into next tr, a V st into next sp, 2 tr into next tr, 1 tr into each of next 18 tr; rep from * omitting 9 tr at end of last rep, 1 ss into 3rd of 3 ch.
10th Row: 3 ch, 1 tr into each of next 10 tr, * 2 tr into next tr, 3 ch, 2 tr into next tr, 1 tr into each of next 22 tr; rep from * omitting 11 tr at end of last rep, 1 ss into 3rd of 3 ch.
11th Row: 3 ch, 1 tr into each of next 11 tr, * 2 tr into next tr, a V st into next sp, 2 tr into next tr, 1 tr into each of next 24 tr; rep from * omitting 12 tr at end of last rep, 1 ss into 3rd of 3 ch.
12th Row: 3 ch, 1 tr into each of next 13 tr, * 2 tr into next tr, 3 ch, 2 tr into next tr, 1 tr into each of next 28 tr; rep from * omitting 14 tr at end of last rep, 1 ss into 3rd of 3 ch.
13th Row: 3 ch, 1 tr into each of next 14 tr, * 2 tr into next tr, a V st into next sp, 2 tr into next tr, 1 tr into each of next 30 tr; rep from * omitting 15 tr at end of last rep, 1 ss into 3rd of 3 ch.
14th Row: 3 ch, 1 tr into each of next 16 tr, * 2 tr into next tr, 3 ch, 2 tr into next tr, 1 tr into each of next 34 tr; rep from * omitting 17 tr at end of last rep, 1 ss into 3rd of 3 ch.
15th Row: 3 ch, 1 tr into each of next 17 tr, * 2 tr into next tr, a V st into next sp, 2 tr into next tr, 1 tr into each of next 36 tr; rep from * omitting 18 tr at end of last rep, 1 ss into 3rd of 3 ch.
16th Row: 3 ch, 1 tr into each of next 19 tr, * 2 tr into next tr, 3 ch, 2 tr into next tr, 1 tr into each of next 40 tr; rep from * omitting 20 tr at end of last rep, 1 ss into 3rd of 3 ch.
17th Row: 3 ch, 1 tr into each of next 20 tr, * 2 tr into next tr, a V st into next sp, 2 tr into next tr, 1 tr into each of next 42 tr; rep from * omitting 21 tr at end of last rep, 1 ss into 3rd of 3 ch. Fasten off.

OVERLAY
1st Row: With right side facing attach C to first lp missed on 2nd row, 3 ch, 4 tr into same lp, * 3 ch, 1 dc into next 1 ch sp on 3rd row, 3 ch, 5 tr into next free lp on 2nd row; rep from * omitting 5 tr at end of last rep, 1 ss into 3rd of 3 ch.
2nd Row: 1 ss into next tr, 1 dc into next tr, * 9 ch, 3 tr into next free 3 ch sp on 5th row, 1 dc into 3 ch sp above on 6th row between 2 tr of V st made on 7th row, 3 tr into same sp on 5th row, 9 ch, 1 dc into centre tr of next 5 tr group; rep from * omitting 9 ch and 1 dc at end of last rep, 4 ch, 1 trip tr into first dc.
3rd Row: 1 dc into lp just formed, 9 ch, 1 dc into next lp, * 9 ch, 3 tr into next 3 ch sp on 7th row, 1 dc into sp above on 8th row between 2 tr of V st made on 9th row, 3 tr into same sp on 7th row, (9 ch, 1 dc into next lp) twice; rep from * omitting (9 ch, 1 dc) twice at end of last rep, 4 ch, 1 trip tr into first dc.
4th Row: 1 dc into lp just formed, * (9 ch, 1 dc into next lp) twice, 9 ch, 3 tr into next sp on 9th row, 1 dc into sp above on 10th row between 2 tr of V st made on 11th row, 3 tr into same sp on 9th row, 9 ch, 1 dc into next lp; rep from * omitting 9 ch and 1 dc at end of last rep, 4 ch, 1 trip tr into first dc.
5th Row: 1 dc into lp just formed, * 9 ch, 1 dc into each of next 2 lps, 9 ch, 1 dc into next lp, 9 ch, 3 tr into next sp on 11th row, 1 dc into sp above on 12th row between 2 tr of V st made on 13th row, 3 tr in same sp on 11th row, 9 ch, 1 dc into next lp; rep from * omitting 9 ch and 1 dc at end of last rep, 4 ch, 1 trip tr into first dc.
6th Row: 1 dc into lp just formed, * 9 ch, 1 dc into next lp, 5 ch, 1 dc into each of next 2 dc, 5 ch, 1 dc into next 9 ch lp, 9 ch, 1 dc into next lp, 9 ch, 3 tr into next sp on 13th row, 1 dc into sp above on 14th row between 2 tr of V st made on 15th row, 3 tr into same sp on 13th row, 9 ch, 1 dc into next lp; rep from * omitting 9 ch and 1 dc at end of last rep, 4 ch, 1 trip tr into first dc.
7th Row: 1 dc into lp just formed, * (9 ch, 1 dc into next lp) twice, 1 dc into next lp, (9 ch, 1 dc into next lp) twice,

9 ch, 3 tr into next sp on 15th row, 1 dc into sp above on 16th row between 2 tr of V st made on 17th row, 3 tr into same sp on 15th row, 9 ch, 1 dc into next lp; rep from * omitting 1 dc at end of last rep, 1 ss into first dc. Fasten off.

EDGING

1st Row: With right side facing attach C to first 3 ch sp made on 17th row, 3 dc into same sp, * 1 dc into each tr, 3 dc into next sp; rep from * ending with 1 dc into each tr, 1 ss into first dc.
2nd Row: 1 dc into same place as ss, 1 dc into each of next 4 dc, * (3 ch, miss 1 dc, 1 dc into next dc) 11 times, (1 dc into next dc, 3 ch, miss 1 dc) 11 times, 1 dc into each of next 7 dc; rep from * omitting 5 dc at end of last rep, 1 ss into first dc.
3rd Row: 1 ss into next dc, 4 ch, 3 dbl tr into same place as last ss, 21 ch, remove lp from hook, insert hook into last dbl tr and draw dropped lp through, 27 dc into lp just made, 1 ss into same dbl tr, 3 dbl tr into same place as last dbl tr, * (1 dc into next lp, 2 ch) 21 times, 1 dc into next lp, miss 3 dc, 7 dbl tr into next dc; rep from * omitting 7 dbl tr at end of last rep, 1 ss into 4th of 4 ch. Fasten off.

Damp and pin out to measurement.

Top for Sweet Jar

MATERIALS: Coats Chain Mercer-Crochet Cotton No. 20: 1 ball selected colour. Milward steel crochet hook 1,25. Hand cut lead crystal jar with 7,5 cm (3″) round silver plated lid approximately 12,5 cm (5″) high suitable for sweets, pot-pourri etc.

TENSION: First 4 rows – 3 cm in diameter.

MEASUREMENT: Finished size of crochet – 12,5 cm in diameter.

ABBREVIATIONS: See p. 3

MAIN SECTION: Commence with 2 ch.
1st Row: 6 dc into 2 nd ch from hook, 1 ss into first dc.
2nd Row: 6 ch, 1 tr into same place as ss, * 3 ch, into next dc work 1 tr 3 ch and 1 tr; rep from * ending with 3 ch, 1 ss into 3rd of 6 ch.

3rd Row: 1 ss into next ch, 1 dc into lp, * 5 ch, 1 dc into next lp; rep from * ending with 5 ch, 1 ss into first dc.
4th Row: 1 dc into same place as ss, * 7 ch, 1 dc into next dc; rep from * ending with 7 ch, 1 ss into first dc.
5th Row: 1 dc into same place as ss, * 9 ch, 1 dc into next dc; rep from * ending with 9 ch, 1 ss into first dc.
6th Row: 1 dc into same place as ss, * 11 ch, 1 dc into next dc; rep from * ending with 11 ch, 1 ss into first dc.
7th Row: Into each lp work 3 dc 5 ch 5 tr 1 hlf tr and 1 dc, 1 ss into first dc.
8th Row: 1 ss into each of next 5 sts, 1 dc into lp, * 5 ch, miss 3 tr, 1 dc into next tr, 5 ch, 1 dc into next lp; rep from * omitting 1 dc at end of last rep, 1 ss into first dc.
9th Row: 1 dc into same place as ss, * 5 dc into next lp, 1 dc into next dc; rep from * ending with 5 dc into next lp, 1 ss into back lp of first dc.
10th Row: 4 ch, working into back lp only of each dc work 1 dbl tr into next dc, 1 ch, miss 1 dc, 1 dbl tr into next dc, 1 ch, miss 1 dc, 1 dbl tr into each of next 2 dc; rep from * omitting 2 dbl tr at end of last rep, 1 ss into 4th of 4 ch.
11th Row: 1 dc into same place as ss, * 3 ch, miss 1 dbl tr, 1 dc into next dbl tr; rep from * ending with 3 ch, 1 ss into first dc.
12th Row: 1 dc into same place as ss, * 5 ch, 1 dc into next dc; rep from * ending with 5 ch, 1 ss into first dc.
13th and 14th Rows: As 4th and 5th rows.
15th Row: Into each lp work 3 dc 3 ch 3 tr 1 hlf tr and 1 dc, 1 ss into first dc. Fasten off.
Damp and pin out to measurement.

TASSEL: Wind thread 150 times round a piece of card 10 cm wide. Secure at top with a 50 ch lp. Remove from card and bind securely 1,5 cm from top.

TASSEL TOP: Commence with 8 ch, join with a ss to form a ring.
1st Row: Into ring work (1 dc, 2 ch) 8 times, 1 ss into first dc.
2nd to 6th Row: 1 ss into first sp, 3 ch, 4 tr into same sp, remove lp from hook, insert hook into 3rd of 3 ch and draw dropped lp through (a starting pc st made), * 2 ch, 5 tr into next sp, remove lp from hook, insert hook into first tr of 5 tr group and draw dropped lp through (a pc st made); rep from * ending with 2 ch, 1 ss into first pc st.
7th Row: * 1 dc into next sp, 2 ch; rep from * ending with 1 ss into first dc. Cut thread leaving sufficient to thread through last row. Place over top of tassel pulling the 50 ch lp through ring. Draw last row up neatly and secure. Cut and trim tassle.

STEM: Commence with 2 ch.
1st Row: 6 dc into 2nd ch from hook, 1 ss into first dc.
2nd Row: 3 ch, 1 tr into each of next 5 dc.
3rd Row: 1 tr round 3 ch, 1 tr round bar of each of next 5 tr.
4th Row: 1 tr round bar of each tr.
Rep 4th row 10 times more ending with 1 ss into next tr. Fasten off.

TO MAKE UP: Using crochet hook draw the 50 ch lp from the tassel through the stem and sew to centre of main section. Sew stem to main section and tassel. Cut a circle of coloured paper 7,5 cm in diameter and place centrally under crochet. Place crochet over jar as shown in illustration.

Coaster

MATERIALS: Coats Ancora Pearl Cotton No. 8 (10g balls): 1 ball each of 059 (Raspberry), 052 (Carnation Pink), 050 (Rose Pink) and 024 (Lt. Rose Pink). This model is worked in these shades, but any other shades of Mercer-Crochet may be used. Milward steel crochet hook 1,50. Two coasters can be worked from 1 ball.

TENSION: First 7 rows – 6,5 cm in diameter.

MEASUREMENT: 15 cm in diameter approximately.
Commence with 6 ch, join with a ss to form a ring.

ABBREVIATIONS: See p. 3

1st Row: 3 ch, 15 tr into ring, 1 ss into 3rd of 3 ch.
2nd Row: 1 dc into same place as ss, * 3 ch, miss 1 tr, 1 dc into next tr; repeat from * ending with 3 ch, 1 ss into first dc.
3rd Row: 1 ss into next loop, 3 ch, 4 tr into same loop, 5 tr into each loop, 1 ss into 3rd of 3 ch.
4th Row: As 2nd row.
5th Row: 1 ss into next loop, 3 ch, 3 tr into same loop, 3 tr into next loop, * 4 tr into next loop, 3 tr into next loop; repeat from * ending with 1 ss into 3rd of 3 ch.
6th Row: As 2nd row.
7th Row: 1 ss into next loop, 3 ch, 1 tr into same loop, * (3 tr into next loop) 4 times, 2 tr into next loop; repeat from * omitting 2 tr at end of last repeat, 1 ss into 3rd of 3 ch.
8th Row: 1 dc into same place as ss, 1 dc into each of next 2 tr, * 13 ch, miss 10 tr, 1 dc into each of next 4 tr; repeat from * omitting 3 dc at end of last repeat, 1 ss into first dc.
9th Row: 1 dc into same place as ss, 1 dc into each of next 2 dc, 8 dc into next loop (11 ch, 1 dc into 2nd ch from hook, 1 hlf tr into next ch, 1 tr into each of next 6 ch, 1 hlf tr into next ch, 1 dc into next ch, 1 ss into next dc – a spoke made, 1 dc into same loop) 3 times, 11 ch, complete a spoke as before (4 spokes completed), 7 dc into same loop, * 1 dc into each of next 4 dc, 8 dc into next loop, 11 ch, remove loop from hook insert hook into dc at tip of last spoke made and draw dropped loop through (a joining st made), 1 dc into 2nd ch from hook and complete a spoke as before, (1 dc into same loop, 11 ch, complete a spoke as before) 3 times, 7 dc into same loop; repeat from * joining last spoke to first spoke to correspond ending with 1 dc into next dc, 1 ss into first dc. Fasten off.
10th Row: With right side facing attach thread to dc at tip of first free spoke on previous row, 1 dc into same place as join, * 9 ch, 1 dc into dc at tip of next spoke, 9 ch, 1 dc into next joining st, 9 ch; 1 dc into dc at tip of next spoke; repeat from * omitting 1 dc at end of last repeat, 1 ss into first dc.
11th Row: Into each loop work 1 dc 1 hlf tr 7 tr 1 hlf tr and 1 dc, 1 ss into first dc. Fasten off.
12th Row: With right side facing and working behind previous 4 rows, attach thread to fourth tr of first 10 tr missed on 7th row, 1 dc into same place as join, 1 dc into each of next 3 tr, * 15 ch, miss first 3 tr of next 10 tr missed on 7th row, 1 dc into each of next 4 tr; repeat from * omitting 4 dc at end of last repeat, 1 ss into first dc.
13th Row: 1 dc into same place as ss, 1 dc into each of next 3 dc, * into next loop work (1 dc, 1 hlf tr, 4 tr, 1 hlf tr) 3 times and 1 dc, 1 dc into each of next 4 dc; repeat from * omitting 4 dc at end of last repeat, 1 ss into first dc.

Fasten off.
Damp and pin out to shape.

ALTERNATIVE SUGGESTIONS: Use these pretty coasters to decorate your pot plants, to complement fragile glassware or to fill with sweets or biscuits.

Pomanders

MATERIALS: Coats Chain Mercer Crochet Cotton No. 40 (20g): 1 ball selected colour. Milward steel crochet hook 1.00 mm, 1 piece of fabric 11 cm x 21 cm for pomander no. 1, 1 piece of fabric 17 cm square for pomander no. 2, 1,60 m Offray Ribbon, 3 mm wide. Pot-pourri or scented cotton wool.

TENSION: First 5 rows – 4,3 cm in diameter.

MEASUREMENTS: Pomander no. 1- 12,5 cm in diameter approximately. Pomander no. 2 – 7 cm high.

ABBREVIATIONS: See p. 3

POMANDER NO. 1

FIRST SECTION: Commence with 8 ch, join with a ss to form a ring.

1st Row: 16 dc into ring, 1 ss into first dc.

2nd Row: 1 dc into same place as ss, * 5 ch, 1 dc into next dc; rep from * ending with 2 ch, 1 tr into first dc.

3rd Row: 1 dc into lp just formed, * 5 ch, 6 tr into next lp, remove lp from hook, insert hook into first tr of tr group and draw dropped lp through (a pc st made), 5 ch, 1 dc into next lp; rep from * omitting 5 ch and 1 dc at end of last rep, 2 ch, 1 tr into first dc.

4th Row: 1 dc into lp just formed, * 5 ch, 1 dc into next lp; rep from * ending with 5 ch, 1 ss into first dc.

5th Row: 1 ss into each of next 2 ch, 1 dc into same lp, * 11 tr into next lp, 1 dc into next lp; rep from * ending with 11 tr into next lp, 1 ss into first dc.

6th Row: 9 ch, 1 dbl tr into same place as ss, * 9 ch, into next dc work 1 dbl tr 5 ch and 1 dbl tr; rep from * ending with 9 ch, 1 ss into 4th of first 9 ch.

7th Row: 1 ss into each of next 2 ch, into same lp work 1 dc 3 ch and 1 dc, * 17 tr into next lp, into next lp work 1 dc 3 ch and 1 dc; rep from * ending with 17 tr into next lp, 1 ss into first dc.

8th Row: 1 ss into next lp, 8 ch, 1 tr into same lp, * 5 ch, miss 5 tr, 1 dc into next tr, (3 ch, miss 1 tr, 1 dc into next tr) 3 times, 5 ch, into next lp work 1 tr 5 ch and 1 tr; rep from * omitting 1 tr 5 ch and 1 tr at end of last rep, 1 ss into 3rd of 8 ch.

9th Row: 1 ss into next ch and into same lp, 2 ch, leaving the last lp of each on hook, work 2 tr into same lp, thread over and draw through all lps on hook (a 2 tr cl made), * 3 ch, a 3 tr cl into next lp; rep from * ending with 3 ch, 1 ss into first cl. Fasten off.

SECOND SECTION: Work as first section. Do not fasten off.

10th Row: 1 ss into next lp, 1 dc into same lp, 5 ch, place first and second sections wrong sides together and working through both sections: 1 dc into next lp, (5 ch, 1 dc into next lp) 30 times, 5 ch, cont to work into second section only: 1 dc into next lp, * 5 ch, 1 dc into next lp; rep from * ending with 1 ch, 1 dbl tr into first dc.

11th Row: Into lp just formed work 1 dc 5 ch and 1 dc, * 5 ch, 1 dc into next lp, 5 ch, into next lp work 1 dc 5 ch and 1 dc; rep from * ending with 5 ch, 1 dc into next lp, 2 ch, 1 tr into first dc.

12th Row: 1 dc into lp just formed, 5 ch, * into next lp work 1 dc 5 ch and 1 dc, (5 ch, 1 dc into next lp) twice, 5 ch; rep from * omitting 5 ch, 1 dc and 5 ch at end of last rep, 2 ch, 1 tr into first dc.

13th and 14th Rows: 1 dc into lp just formed, * 5 ch, 1 dc into next lp; rep from * ending with 2 ch, 1 tr into first dc.

15th Row: 1 dc into lp just formed, * (4 ch, 1 dc into next lp) twice, 9 tr-into next lp, 1 dc into next lp; rep from * omitting 1 dc at end of last rep, 1 ss into first dc. Fasten off. Damp and pin out to shape.

TO MAKE UP: 5 mm has been allowed for seams. Cut 2 circles from fabric 9,5 cm in diameter. Place circles' right sides together and stitch round on seam line leaving an opening for stuffing. Turn to right side, fill with lavender or as desired and sew opening. Insert pad in thread ribbon through 8th row of second crochet section and tie neatly in a bow.

POMANDER NO. 2 (make 2)

Work as first section of pomander no. 1 for 8 rows.

9th Row: 1 ss into each of next 2 ch, 1 dc into same lp, * 3 ch, 1 dc into next lp; rep from * ending with 3 ch, 1 ss into first dc.

10th and 11th Rows: 1 ss into next ch, 1 dc into same lp, * 3 ch, 1 dc into next lp; rep from * ending with 1 ss into first dc.

12th Row: 1 ss into next ch, 1 dc into same lp, * 5 ch, leaving the last lp of each on hook work 1 dbl tr into each of next 2 lps, thread over and draw through all lps on hook (a joint st made), 5 ch, 1 dc into next lp; rep from * omitting 1 dc at end of last rep, 1 ss into first dc.

13th Row: 1 ss into each of next 5 ch and into next joint st, 9 ch, 1 dbl tr into same place as last ss, * 5 ch, into next joint st work 1 dbl tr 5 ch and 1 dbl tr; rep from * ending with 2 ch, 1 tr into 4th of 9 ch.

14th and 15th Rows: 1 dc into lp just formed, * 4 ch, 1 dc into next lp; rep from * ending with 1 ch, 1 tr into first dc.

16th Row: 1 dc into lp just formed, * 4 ch, 1 dc into next lp; rep from * ending with 4 ch, 1 ss into first dc.

17th Row: 1 ss into next lp, 2 ch, leaving the last lp of each on hook work 2 tr into same lp, thread over and draw through all lps on hook (a 2 tr cl made), * 4 ch, a 3 tr cl into next lp; rep from * ending with 1 ch, 1 tr into first cl.

18th to 23rd Row: As 14th row.

24th Row: As 16th row.

25th Row: 1 ss into each of next 2 ch, 1 dc into same lp, * 9 tr into next lp, 1 dc into next lp; rep from * ending with 9 tr into next lp, 1 ss into first dc. Fasten off.

TO MAKE UP: Cut a circule from fabric 16 cm in diamater. Make a line of gathering stitches 3 mm from raw edge and draw up gathers leaving an opening for stuffing. Fill with lavender or as desired and close opening tucking in raw edge and secure. Place inside crochet. Thread ribbon through 17th row and tie neatly in a bow as shown in illustration and decorate as desired.

Doily

MATERIALS: Coats Ancora Pearl Cotton No. 8 (10 g): 2 balls 0292 (Lt. Cream) and 1 ball each of 028 (Indian Pink), 027 (Coral Pink), 054 (Cerise), 0330 (Orange), 0131 (Lt. Peacock Blue), 0211 (Dk. Moss Green) and 0257 (Lt. Moss Green). This model is worked in these eight shades, but any other shades of Mercer-Crochet may be used. Milward steel crochet hook 1,25 mm.

TENSION: First row of large centre flower – 2,5 cm (1 in) in diameter.

MEASUREMENT: 33 cm (13 in) in diameter.

ABBREVIATIONS: See p. 3

LARGE CENTRE FLOWER: Using Indian Pink commence with 14 ch, join with a ss to form a ring.
1st Row: * Into ring work 1 ss 4 ch, leaving the last loop of each on hook work 3 dbl tr, thread over and draw through all loops on hook (a 3 dbl tr cluster made), 4 ch; repeat from * 7 times more, 1 ss into ring. Fasten off.
2nd Row: Attach Coral Pink to first cluster, 1 dc into same place as join, * 6 ch, 1 dc into next cluster; repeat from * ending with 6 ch, 1 ss into first dc.
3rd Row: Into each loop work 1 dc 1 hlf tr 5 tr 1 hlf tr and 1 dc, 1 ss into first dc.
4th Row: * 7 ch, 1 dc into next dc on 2nd row inserting hook from behind; repeat from * ending with 7 ch.
5th Row: Into each loop work 1 dc 1 hlf tr 7 tr 1 hlf tr and 1 dc; 1 ss into first dc.
6th Row: * 8 ch, 1 dc into next dc on 4th row inserting hook from behind; repeat from * ending with 8 ch.
7th Row: Into each loop work 1 dc 1 half tr 9 tr 1 hlf tr and 1 dc; 1 ss into first dc.
8th Row: * 9 ch, 1 dc into next dc on 6th row inserting hook from behind; repeat from * ending with 9 ch.
9th Row: Into each loop work 1 dc 1 hlf tr 10 tr 1 hlf tr and 1 dc; 1 ss into first dc.
10th Row: (14 ch, 1 dc into next dc on 8th row inserting hook from behind) 5 times, (17 ch, 1 dc into next dc on 8th row inserting hook from behind) twice, 17 ch.
11th Row: (15 dc into next loop) 5 times, (19 dc into next loop) 3 times, 1 ss into first dc.
12th Row: 1 ss into next dc, * (1 dc into next dc, 3 ch, miss 1 dc) 5 times, 1 dc into next dc, 1 ss into each of next 4 dc; repeat from * 4 times more, ** (1 dc into next dc, 3 ch, miss 1 dc) 7 times, 1 dc into next dc, 1 ss into each of next 4 dc; repeat from ** twice more omitting 2 ss at end of last repeat. Fasten off.

FIRST SMALL FLOWER: Using Orange commence with 8 ch, join with a ss to form a ring.
1st Row: 12 dc into ring, 1 ss into back loop of first dc.
2nd Row: 1 dc into same place as ss, * 3 ch, miss 1 dc, 1 dc into back loop of next dc; repeat from * ending with 3 ch, 1 ss into first dc.
3rd Row: Into each loop work 1 dc 1 hlf tr 3 tr 1 hlf tr and 1 dc; 1 ss into first dc.
4th Row: 1 ch, * 1 dc into back loop of next free dc on 1st row inserting hook from behind, 5 ch; repeat from * 5 times more.
5th Row: Into each loop work 1 dc 1 hlf tr 5 tr 1 hlf tr and 1 dc; 1 ss into first dc.
6th Row: 1 dc into next st, 3 ch, miss 2 sts, 1 dc into next st, 1 ch, miss first 6 loops made on 12th row of large centre flower, 1 dc into next loop, 1 ch, 1 dc into same st on first small flower, 3 ch, miss 2 sts, 1 dc into next st, 1 ss into each of next 2 dc, 1 dc into next st, 3 ch, miss 2 sts, 1 dc into next st, 1 ch, miss 2 loops to left of last join on large centre flower, 1 dc into next loop, 1 ch, 1 dc into same st on first small flower, * 3 ch, miss 2 sts, 1 dc into next st, 1 ss into each of next 2 dc, 1 dc into next st, 3 ch, miss 2 sts, into next st work 1 dc 3 ch and 1 dc; repeat from * ending with 3 ch, miss 2 sts, 1 dc into next st, 1 ss into next st. Fasten off.

SECOND SMALL FLOWER: Using Lt. Peacock Blue commence with 7 ch.
1st Row: Into 7th ch from hook work (1 tr, 3 ch) 5 times, 1 ss into 4th of 7 ch.
2nd Row: Into each sp work 1 dc 1 hlf tr 3 tr 1 hlf tr and 1 dc; 1 ss into first dc.
3rd Row: 1 dc into next st, 3 ch, miss 1 st, 1 dc into next st, 1 ch, miss two 3 ch loops to left of last join on first small flower, 1 dc into next loop, 1 ch, 1 dc into same st on second small flower, 3 ch, miss 1 st, 1 dc into next st, 1 ss into each of next 2 dc, 1 dc into next st, 3 ch, miss 1 st, 1 dc into next st, 1 ch, miss 1 loop on large centre flower, 1 dc into next loop, 1 ch, 1 dc into same st on second small flower, 3 ch, miss 1 st, 1 dc into next st, 1 ss into each of next 2 dc, 1 dc into next st, 3 ch, miss 1 dc, 1 dc into next st, 1 ch, miss 2 loops on large centre flower, 1 dc into next loop, 1 ch, 1 dc into same st on second small flower, * 3 ch, miss 1 st, 1 dc into next st, 1 ss into each of next 2 dc, 1 dc into next st, 3 ch, miss 1 st, into next st work 1 dc 3 ch and 1 dc; repeat from * ending with 3 ch, miss 1 st, 1 dc into next st, 1 ss into next dc. Fasten off.

THIRD SMALL FLOWER: Using Cerise commence with 14 ch, join with a ss to form a ring.
1st Row: Into ring work 1 dc 1 hlf tr and 2 tr, miss 1 loop on large centre flower, 1 ss into next loop, into ring on third small flower work 1 tr 1 hlf tr 1 dc 1 hlf tr 3 tr 1 hlf tr 1 dc (1 ss, 4 ch, a 3 dbl tr cluster, 4 ch) 4 times, 1 ss 1 dc 1 hlf tr 3 tr and 1 hlf tr; 1 ss into first dc. Fasten off.

FOURTH SMALL FLOWER: Using Orange commence with 8 ch, join with a ss to form a ring.
1st Row: 4 ch, a 3 dbl tr cluster into ring, miss 4 loops on large centre flower, 1 ss into next loop, 4 ch, into ring of fourth small flower work (1 ss, 4 ch, a 3 dbl tr cluster, 4 ch) 4 times and 1 ss. Fasten off.

FIFTH SMALL FLOWER: Using Cerise work as fourth small flower joining to large centre flower in same manner missing 3 loops on large centre flower instead of 4 loops.

SIXTH SMALL FLOWER: Using Orange work as third small flower joining to large centre flower in same manner missing 4 loops on large centre flower instead of 1 loop.

SEVENTH SMALL FLOWER: Using Cerise work as second small flower for 2 rows.
3rd Row: 1 dc into next st, 3 ch, miss 1 st, 1 dc into next st, 1 ch, miss 1 loop on large centre flower, 1 dc into next loop, 1 ch, 1 dc into same st on seventh small flower, 3 ch, miss 1 st, 1 dc into next st, 1 ss into each of next 2 dc, 1 dc into next st, 3 ch, miss 1 st, 1 dc into next st, 1 ch, miss 2 loops on large centre flower, 1 dc into next loop, 1 ch, 1 dc into same st on seventh small flower and complete as second small flower.

EIGHTH SMALL FLOWER: Using Lt. Peacock Blue work as first small flower joining to seventh small flower and large centre flower to correspond with first and second small flowers.

FIRST LEAF: Using Lt. Moss Green commence with 15 ch.
1st Row: 1 dc into 2nd ch from hook, 1 dc into each ch to within last ch, into next ch work 1 dc 3 ch and 1 dc (tip of leaf), 1 dc into each ch along opposite side of foundation ch, 1 dc into same place as last dc (base of leaf). Hereafter pick up only the back loop of each dc, 1 dc into each of next 11 dc, 1 ch, turn.
2nd Row: Miss two 3 ch loops to left of last join on eighth small flower, 1 dc into next loop, 1 ch, 1 dc into each dc on leaf to within centre dc of 3 dc group at base of leaf, 3 dc into next dc, 1 dc into each dc on other side to within 4 dc from 3 ch loop at tip of leaf, 3 ch, turn.
3rd and 4th Rows: 1 dc into each dc to within centre dc of 3 dc group at base of leaf, 3 dc into next dc, 1 dc into each dc to within last 3 dc, 3 ch, turn.
5th Row: 1 dc into each dc to within centre dc of 3 dc group at base of leaf, into next dc work 1 dc 7 ch and 1 dc, 1 dc into each dc to within last 3 dc, 1 ch, turn.
6th Row: Miss 1 loop on large centre flower, 1 dc into next loop, 1 ch, 1 dc into each dc on leaf to within 7 ch loop, 2 dc into loop, 1 ch, miss 2 loops on large centre flower, 1 dc into next loop, 1 ch, into loop on leaf work 3 dc 3 ch 3 dc 3 ch and 2 dc; 1 dc into each dc to within last 3 dc, 3 ch, 1 ss into same place as last dc. Fasten off.

SECOND LEAF: Using Dk. Moss Green work as first leaf for 1 row turning with 3 ch instead of 1 ch.
2nd Row: 1 dc into each dc to within centre dc of 3 dc group at base of leaf, 3 dc into next dc, 1 dc into each dc on other side to within 4 dc from 3 ch loop at tip of leaf, 1 ch, turn.
3rd Row: With wrong side of previous motifs facing miss 2 loops to left of first join of first small flower, 1 dc into next loop, 1 ch, 1 dc into each dc on leaf to within centre dc of 3 dc group at base of leaf, 3 dc into next dc, 1 dc into each dc to within last 3 dc, 3 ch, turn.
4th and 5th Rows: As 4th and 5th rows of first leaf turning with 3 ch instead of 1 ch at end of 5th row.
6th Row: 1 dc into each dc to within 7 ch loop, into loop work 2 dc 3 ch 3 dc 3 ch and 3 dc, 1 ch, miss 1 loop on large centre flower, 1 dc into next loop, 1 ch, 2 dc into same loop on leaf, 1 dc into each dc to within last 3 dc, 1 ch, miss 2 loops on large centre flower, 1 dc into next loop, 1 ch, 1 ss into same place as last dc on leaf. Fasten off.

NINTH SMALL FLOWER: Work as first small flower for 1 row.
2nd Row: 4 ch, a 3 dbl tr cluster into same place as ss, 1 ch, 1 dc into second free 3 ch loop to left of last join on first leaf, 1 ch, 1 ss into top of last cluster on ninth small flower, 4 ch, 1 ss into same place as cluster, 1 ss into back loop of each of next 2 dc, 4 ch, a 3 dbl tr cluster into same place as last ss, 1 ch, 1 dc into second free 3 ch loop to right of second join on second leaf, 1 ch, 1 ss into top of last cluster on ninth small flower, 4 ch, 1 ss into same place as last cluster, * 1 ss into back loop of next dc, into back loop of next dc work 1 ss 4 ch a 3 dbl tr cluster 3 ch 1 ss into last cluster – a picot made – 4 ch and 1 ss; repeat from * ending with 1 ss into back loop of next dc. Fasten off.

EDGING
1st Row: With right side facing attach Lt. Cream to third free picot to right of first join on ninth small flower, 1 dc into same place as join, 8 ch, 1 dc into next picot, 8 ch, 1 trip tr into next picot, 8 ch, 1 quad tr into first free 3 ch loop on next leaf, 8 ch, 1 trip tr into next 3 ch loop on leaf, 8 ch, 1 dbl tr into next 3 ch loop on leaf, 8 ch, 1 dbl tr into 3 ch loop at tip of leaf, 8 ch, miss 2 loops on next flower, 1 dc into next loop, 8 ch, miss 2 loops, 1 dc into next loop, 8 ch, 1 quad tr into join of seventh and eighth small flowers, 8 ch, miss 2 loops on seventh small flower, 1 dc into next loop, 8 ch, miss 2 loops, 1 dc into next loop, 8 ch, * miss 1 cluster on next flower, (1 tr into next cluster, 8 ch) twice; repeat from * 3 times more, miss 5 loops on next flower, 1 dc into next loop, 8 ch, miss 2 loops, 1 dc into next loop, 8 ch, 1 quad tr into join of first and second small flowers, 8 ch, miss 2 loops on first small flower, 1 dc into next loop, 8 ch, miss 2 loops, 1 dc into next loop, 8 ch, 1 dbl tr into 3 ch loop at tip of next leaf, 8 ch, 1 dbl tr into next 3 ch loop, 8 ch, 1 trip tr into next 3 ch loop, 8 ch, 1 quad tr into next 3 ch loop, 8 ch, 1 trip tr into first free picot on ninth small flower, 3 ch, 1 trip tr into first dc.
2nd Row: 1 dc into loop just formed, * 9 ch, 1 dc into next loop; repeat from * ending with 9 ch, 1 ss into first dc.
3rd Row: Into each loop work 1 dc 1 hlf tr 9 tr 1 hlf tr and 1 dc, 1 ss into first dc.
4th Row: 1 ss into each of next 3 sts, 1 dc into same place as last ss, * 5 ch, miss 5 tr, 1 dc into next tr, 7 ch, miss 6 sts, 1 dc into next tr; repeat from * omitting 1 dc at end of last repeat, 1 ss into first dc.
5th Row: 1 ss into next loop, 3 ch, into same loop work 1 dbl tr 5 ch and a 2 dbl tr cluster, * 3 ch, into next loop work 1 dc 3 ch and 1 ss into last dc (another picot made), 3 ch, into next loop work a 2 dbl tr cluster 5 ch and a 2 dbl tr cluster; repeat from * omitting a cluster 5 ch and a cluster at end of last repeat, 1 ss into first dbl tr.
6th Row: 1 ss into next ch and into loop, into same loop work 1 dc 3 ch and 1 dc, * 3 ch, 1 dc into next loop, 7 ch, 1 dc into next loop, 3 ch, into next loop work 1 dc 3 ch and 1 dc; repeat from * omitting 1 dc 3 ch and 1 dc at end of last repeat, 1 ss into first dc.
7th Row: 1 ss into next loop, 3 ch, into same loop work 1 dbl tr 5 ch and a 2 dbl tr cluster, * 3 ch, into next 7 ch loop work 1 dc and a picot, 3 ch, miss

1 loop, into next loop work a 2 dbl tr cluster 5 ch and a 2 dbl tr cluster; repeat from * omitting a cluster 5 ch and a cluster at end of last repeat, 1 ss into first dbl tr. Repeat 6th and 7th rows once more then 6th row again.

11th Row: 1 ss into next loop, 3 ch, into same loop work 1 dbl tr 5 ch and a 2 dbl tr cluster, * 4 ch, into next 7 ch loop work 1 dc and a picot, 4 ch, miss 1 loop, into next loop work a 2 dbl tr cluster 5 ch and a 2 dbl tr cluster; repeat from * omitting a cluster 5 ch and a cluster at end of last repeat, 1 ss into first dbl tr.

12th Row: 1 ss into next ch and into loop, into same loop work 1 dc 3 ch and 1 dc, * 3 ch, 1 dc into next loop, 8 ch, 1 dc into next loop, 3 ch, into next loop work 1 dc 3 ch and 1 dc; repeat from * omitting 1 dc 3 ch and 1 dc at end of last repeat, 1 ss into first dc.

13th Row: 1 ss into next loop, 3 ch, into same loop work 1 dbl tr 5 ch and a 2 dbl tr cluster, * 5 ch, into next 8 ch loop work 1 dc and a picot, 5 ch, miss 1 loop, into next loop work a 2 dbl tr cluster 5 ch and a 2 dbl tr cluster; repeat from * omitting a cluster 5 ch and a cluster at end of last repeat, 1 ss into first dbl tr.

14th Row: 1 ss into next ch and into loop, into same loop work 1 dc 3 ch and 1 dc, * 3 ch, 1 dc into next loop, 9 ch, 1 dc into next loop, 3 ch, into next loop work 1 dc 3 ch and 1 dc; repeat from * omitting 1 dc 3 ch and 1 dc at end of last repeat, 1 ss into first dc.

15th Row: 1 ss into next loop, 3 ch, into same loop work 1 dbl tr 5 ch and a 2 dbl tr cluster, * 6 ch, into next 9 ch loop work 1 dc and a picot, 6 ch, miss 1 loop, into next loop work a 2 dbl tr cluster 5 ch and a 2 dbl tr cluster; repeat from * omitting a cluster 5 ch and a cluster at end of last repeat, 1 ss into first dbl tr.

16th Row: 1 ss into each of next 2 ch, 1 dc into loop, * 10 ch, leaving the last loop of each on hook work 1 quad tr into each of next 2 loops thread over and draw through all loops on hook (a joint quad tr made), 10 ch, 1 dc into next loop; repeat from * omitting 1 dc at end of last repeat, 1 ss into first dc.

17th Row: * Into next loop work 1 dc 1 hlf tr 6 tr a picot and 4 tr, into next joint st work 2 tr a picot and 1 tr, into next loop work 5 tr a picot 5 tr 1 hlf tr and 1 dc; repeat from * ending with 1 ss into first dc. Fasten off.

Damp and pin out to measurements.

All set

MATERIALS: Coats Chain Mercer-Crochet Cotton No. 20 (20 g): 1 ball White and 2 balls 442 (Mid Buttercup). This model is worked in these two shades, but any shades of Mercer-Crochet may be used. Milward steel crochet hook 1,25 mm. Two buttons. The above quantity is sufficient for 2 place mats, 2 glass mats and 2 napkin holders.

ABBREVIATIONS: See p. 3

TENSION: First 6 rows of place mat – 7,5 cm (3 in) in diameter.

MEASUREMENTS: Place mat – 18,5 cm ($7\frac{1}{4}$ in) in diameter. Glass mat – 11 cm ($4\frac{1}{4}$ in) in diameter. Napkin Holder: Length of Band – 13 cm (5 in).

PLACE MAT: Using White commence with 10 ch, join with a ss to form a ring.

1st Row: 16 dc into ring, 1 ss into first dc.

2nd Row: 1 dc into same place as ss, * 13 ch, miss 1 dc, 1 dc into next dc; repeat from * ending with 13 ch, 1 ss into first dc. Fasten off.

3rd Row: Using Mid Buttercup and working behind previous row, attach thread to first free dc on 1st row, 1 dc into same place as join, * 17 ch, 1 dc into next free dc on 1st row; repeat from * ending with 17 ch, 1 ss into first dc.

4th Row: 1 ss into each of next 9 ch, 1 dc into same loop, * 9 ch, 1 dc into next loop on 2nd row, 9 ch, 1 dc into next loop on 3rd row; repeat from * omitting 1 dc at end of last repeat, 1 ss into first dc.

5th Row: 2 ch, 1 tr into each of next 4 ch, * 5 ch, 1 dc into next ch, 3 ch, miss 4 ch on next loop, 1 dc into next ch, 5 ch, 1 tr into each of next 3 ch, leaving the last loop of each on hook work 1 tr into each of next 3 sts, thread over and draw through all loops on hook (a cluster made), 1 tr into each of next 3 ch; repeat from * omitting a cluster and 3 tr at end of last repeat, leaving the last loop on hook work 1 tr into next ch, insert hook into first tr and draw through all loops on hook.

6th Row: 1 ss into each of next 3 tr and into next loop, 1 dc into same loop, * 9 ch, 1 dc into next 5 ch loop; repeat from * ending with 9 ch, 1 ss into first dc.

7th Row: 1 ss into each of next 5 ch, 1 dc into same loop, * 3 ch, into next loop work 7 tr 3 ch and 7 tr, 3 ch, 1 dc into next loop; repeat from * omitting 1 dc at end of last repeat, 1 ss into first dc. Fasten off.

8th Row: Using White, attach thread to first loop made on previous row, 1 dc into same place as join, * 9 ch, 1 dc into next loop, 9 ch, 1 dc into next loop, 5 ch, 1 dc into next loop; repeat from * omitting 5 ch and 1 dc at end of last repeat, 2 ch, 1 tr into first dc.

9th Row: 17 ch, * 1 dc into next loop, 7 ch, 1 dc into next loop, 11 ch, 1 quad tr into next loop, 11 ch; repeat from * omitting 1 quad tr and 11 ch at end of last repeat, 1 ss into 6th of 17 ch.

10th Row: 1 ss into each of next 4 ch, 1 dc into same loop, * (11 ch, 1 dc into next loop) twice, 9 ch, 1 dc into next loop; repeat from * omitting 1 dc at end of last repeat, 1 ss into first dc. Fasten off.

11th Row: Using Mid Buttercup, attach thread to any 9 ch loop on previous row, 1 dc into same place as join, * 7 ch, 1 dc into next loop, 11 ch, leaving the last loop of each on hook work 1 quad tr into same loop as last dc and into next loop, thread over and draw through all loops on hook (a joint quad tr made), 11 ch, 1 dc into same loop as last quad tr, 7 ch, 1 dc into next loop; repeat from * omitting 7 ch and 1 dc at end of last repeat, 3 ch, 1 dbl tr into first dc.

12th Row: 1 dc into loop just formed, * 7 ch, 1 dc into next loop, 13 dbl tr into next loop, 1 dbl tr into next joint st, 13 dbl tr into next loop, 1 dc into next loop; repeat from * omitting 1 dc at end of last repeat, 1 ss into first dc.

13th Row: * Into next loop work 1 dc 7 ch and 1 dc, miss 1 dbl tr, 1 dc into next dbl tr, (11 ch, miss 3 dbl tr, 1 dc into next dbl tr) 6 times; repeat from * ending with 1 ss into first dc. Drop Mid Buttercup but do not fasten off.

14th Row: Using White and working in front of previous row, attach thread to 7 ch loop on 12th row between first and second dc made on 13th row, 1 dc into same place as join, * 9 ch, (1 dc into centre dbl tr of next 3 dbl tr missed on 12th row, 11 ch) 5 times, 1 dc into centre dbl tr of next 3 dbl tr missed on 12th row, 9 ch, 1 dc into next 7 ch loop on 12th row; repeat from * omitting 1 dc at end of last repeat, 1 ss into first dc. Fasten off White.

15th Row: Pick up Mid Buttercup, 1 ss into each of next 3 ch of 7 ch loop on 13th row, 1 dc into same loop, * 3 dc into next loop on 14th row, (4 dc into next loop on 13th row, 4 dc into next loop on 14th row) 5 times, 4 dc into next loop on 13th row, 3 dc into next loop on 14th row, 1 dc into next loop on 13th row; repeat from * omitting 1 dc at end of last repeat, 1 ss into first dc. Fasten off.

GLASS MAT: Work as place mat for 6 rows.

7th Row: 1 ss into each of next 5 ch, 1 dc into same loop, * 3 ch, 15 tr into next loop, 3 ch, 1 dc into next loop; repeat from * omitting 1 dc at end of last repeat, 1 ss into first dc.

8th Row: 1 ss into each of next 2 ch, 1 dc into same loop, * (7 ch, miss 3 tr, 1 dc into next tr) 3 times, 7 ch, 1 dc into next loop, 5 ch, 1 dc into next loop; repeat from * omitting 1 dc at end of last repeat, 1 ss into first dc. Drop Mid Buttercup but do not fasten off.

9th Row: Using White and working in front of previous row, attach thread to same dc as last ss on 7th row, 1 dc into same place as join, * 6 ch, 1 dc into centre tr of next 3 tr missed on 7th row, (7 ch, 1 dc into centre tr of next 3 tr missed on 7th row) 3 times, 6 ch, 1 dc into next dc on 7th row; repeat from * omitting 1 dc at end of last repeat, 1 ss into first dc. Fasten off.

10th Row: Pick up Mid Buttercup, 1 ss into each of next 2 ch on 8th row, 4 dc into same loop, * (4 dc into next loop on 9th row, 4 dc into next loop on 8th row) 3 times, 1 dc into next loop on 9th row, 1 dc into next loop on 8th row, 1 dc into next loop on 9th row, 4 dc into next loop on 8th row; repeat from * omitting 4 dc at end of last repeat, 1 ss into first dc. Fasten off.

NAPKIN HOLDER

BAND: Using Mid Buttercup commence with 61 ch.

1st Row: (right side): 1 tr into 4th ch from hook, 1 tr into each ch, 1 ch, turn.

2nd Row: 1 dc into each st, 3 ch, turn.

3rd Row: Working into back loop only of each dc, miss first dc, 1 tr into each dc. Fasten off but do not turn.

4th Row: Attach White to top of last tr, 2 dc into same place as join, 3 dc over last row end, 1 dc over next row end, 3 dc over next row end, 2 dc into same ch as tr, 3 ch, and continuing to work along foundation ch, * miss next ch, 1 dc into next ch, 3 ch; repeat from * along foundation ch ending with miss next ch, 2 dc into next ch, 3 dc over row end, 1 dc over next row end, 3 dc over next row end, 2 dc into top of turning ch **, 3 ch, miss 1 tr, 1 dc into next tr; repeat from ** ending with 3 ch, miss 1 tr, 1 ss into first dc, 1 ss into each of next 2 dc, 7 ch, miss 5 dc, 1 ss into next dc (button loop made). Fasten off.

FRILL

1st Row (wrong side): With right side facing and working into front loop only of each dc, miss first 5 dc on 2nd row of band, attach Mid Buttercup to next dc, 1 dc into same place as join, 5 ch, miss 2 dc, 1 dc into next dc, 11 ch, miss 2 dc, a joint quad tr into next dc, miss 4 dc and into next dc, 11 ch, miss 2 dc, 1 dc into next dc, 5 ch, miss 3 dc, 1 dc into next dc, 11 ch, miss 2 dc, a joint quad tr into next dc, miss 5 dc and into next dc, 11 ch, miss 2 dc, 1 dc into next dc, 5 ch, miss 3 dc, 1 dc into next dc, 11 ch, miss 2 dc, a joint quad tr into next dc, miss 4 dc and into next dc, 11 ch, miss 2 dc, 1 dc into next dc, 3 ch, miss 2 dc, 1 hlf tr into next dc, 1 ch, turn.

2nd Row: 1 dc into loop just formed, * 13 dbl tr into next loop, 1 dbl tr into next joint st, 13 dbl tr into next loop, 1 dc into next loop; repeat from * ending with 1 ch, turn.

3rd Row: Miss first dbl tr, * 1 dc into next dbl tr, (11 ch, miss 3 dbl tr, 1 dc into next dbl tr) 6 times, miss 2 dbl tr; repeat from * missing 1 dbl tr at end of last repeat, 1 ss into next dc, 1 ch, turn. Drop Mid Buttercup but do not fasten off.

4th Row: Using White and working in front of previous row, attach thread to centre dbl tr of first 3 dbl tr missed on 2nd row, 1 dc into same place as join, * (11 ch, 1 dc into centre dbl tr of next 3 dbl tr missed on 2nd row) 5 times, 9 ch, 1 dc into centre dbl tr of next 3 dbl tr missed on 2nd row; repeat from * omitting 9 ch and 1 dc at end of last repeat. Fasten off.

5th Row: With right side of frill facing, using Mid Buttercup, and working into last 2 rows alternately as before work 8 dc into first loop, * 4 dc into each of next 10 loops, 2 dc into next loop, 4 dc into next loop; repeat from * twice more omitting 6 dc at end of last repeat, 8 dc into next loop, 1 ss into next dc. Fasten off.

Damp and pin out to measurements. Sew on button to correspond with button loop.

Glass Mats

MATERIALS: Coats Chain Mercer-Crochet Cotton No. 20 (20 g): 2 balls 901 (Shaded Yellow) and 1 ball 608 (Lt. Cream). This model is worked in these shades but any other shades of Mercer-Crochet may be used. Milward steel crochet hook 1,25 mm. Make six.

TENSION: First row – 2,7 cm in diameter.

MEASUREMENT: 10,5 cm in diameter. Using Lt. Cream commence with 16 ch, join with a ss to form a ring.

ABBREVIATIONS: See p. 3

1st Row: 3 ch, leaving the last loop of each on hook work 2 dbl tr into ring, thread over and draw through all loops on hook (a 2 dbl tr cluster made), 4 ch, into ring work (a 3 dbl tr cluster, 4 ch) 11 times, 1 ss into first cluster.
2nd Row: * Into next loop work 3 dc 25 ch and 3 dc, 5 dc into next loop; repeat from * ending with 1 ss into first dc.
3rd Row: 1 dc into same place as ss, * 31 tr into next loop, miss 2 dc, 1 dc into each of next 7 dc; repeat from * omitting 1 dc at end of last repeat, 1 ss into first dc. Fasten off.
4th Row: With right side facing attach Shaded Yellow to 3rd tr made on previous row, 2 ch, * 1 tr into each of next 3 tr, 3 tr into next tr, 1 tr into each of next 4 tr, 1 hlf tr into next tr, 2 dc into each of next 7 tr, 1 hlf tr into next tr, 1 tr into each of next 4 tr, 3 tr into next tr, 1 tr into each of next 3 tr, 1 hlf tr into next tr, miss 4 sts, leaving the last loop of each on hook work 1 tr into each of next 3 dc, thread over and draw through all loops on hook (a 3 tr cluster made) miss 4 sts, 1 hlf tr into next tr; repeat from * omitting 1 hlf tr at end of last repeat, 1 ss into 2nd of 2 ch.
5th Row: 1 ss into each of next 3 tr, * 1 dc into each of next 7 tr, 2 dc into next hlf tr, 1 dc into each of next 14 dc, 2 dc into next hlf tr, 1 dc into each of next 7 tr, miss 4 sts, 1 dbl tr into next cluster, miss 4 sts; repeat from * ending with 1 ss into first dc.
6th Row: 1 ss into each of next 2 dc, * 1 dc into each of next 26 dc, miss 3 dc, 4 dbl tr into next dbl tr, miss 3 dc; repeat from * ending with 1 ss into first dc.
7th Row: 1 ss into each of next 2 dc, * 1 dc into each of next 20 dc, miss 3 dc, 2 dbl tr into next dbl tr, 1 dbl tr into each of next 2 dbl tr, 2 dbl tr into next dbl tr, miss 3 dc; repeat from * ending with 1 ss into first dc.
8th Row: 1 ss into each of next 2 dc, * (1 dc into next dc, 2 ch) 13 times, 1 dc into next dc, miss 3 dc, 2 dbl tr into each of next 6 dbl tr, miss 3 dc; repeat from * ending with 1 ss into first dc. Fasten off.
Work five more mats in same manner.

Damp and pin out to measurement.

Jam Pot Covers

MATERIALS: Coats Chain Mercer-Crochet Cotton No. 20 (20 g): 1 ball. These models are worked in White, but any shade of Mercer-Crochet may be used. Milward steel crochet hook 1,25 mm. Length of narrow ribbon sufficient to fit round neck of each jar and tie in a bow. The above quantity is sufficient for 2 covers of each design.

TENSION: Cover No. 1 – First 2 rows – 3,5 cm in diameter. Cover No. 2 – First 3 rows – 4,5 cm in diameter.

MEASUREMENTS: Cover No. 1 – To fit jar top – 6,5 cm in diameter. Cover No. 2 – To fit most sizes of jar tops.

ABBREVIATIONS: See p. 3

COVER NO. 1: Commence with 7 ch, join with a ss to form a ring.
1st Row: 3 ch, 17 tr into ring, 1 ss into 3rd of 3 ch.
2nd Row: 3 ch, 1 dbl tr into same place as ss, * 3 ch, leaving the last loop of each on hook work 2 dbl tr into next tr, thread over and draw through all loops on hook (a 2 dbl tr cluster made); repeat from * ending with 3 ch, 1 ss into first dbl tr.
3rd Row: 1 ss into next ch, 1 dc into same loop, * 4 ch, 1 dc into next loop; repeat from * ending with 1 ch, 1 tr into first dc.
4th Row: 1 dc into loop just formed, * 5 ch, 1 dc into next loop; repeat from * ending with 5 ch, 1 ss into first dc.
5th Row: Into each loop work 2 dc 3 ch and 2 dc, 1 ss into first dc.
6th Row: 1 ss into next dc, * 3 dc into next loop, 3 ch; repeat from * ending with 1 ss into first dc.
7th Row: 1 ss into front loop of next dc, 3 ch, 6 tr into same dc, * 1 dc into next loop, miss 1 dc, 7 tr into front loop of next dc; repeat from * ending with 1 dc into next loop, 1 ss into 3rd of 3 ch. Fasten off.
8th Row: With right side facing and working behind previous row, attach thread to back loop of second dc made on 6th row, 1 dc into same place as join, * 5 ch, miss 2 dc on 6th row, 1 dc into back loop of next dc; repeat from * ending with 5 ch, 1 ss into first dc.
9th Row: 3 ch, * 5 tr into next loop, 1 tr into next dc; repeat from * ending with 5 tr into next loop, 1 ss into 3rd of 3 ch.
10th Row: 2 ch, 1 tr into same place as ss, * 5 ch, miss 5 tr, a 2 tr cluster into next tr; repeat from * einding with 5 ch, 1 ss into first tr.
11th Row: 1 dc into same place as ss, * 7 ch, 1 dc into next cluster; repeat from * ending with 7 ch, 1 ss into first dc.
12th Row: Into each loop work 1 dc 1 hlf tr 5 tr 1 hlf tr and 1 dc, 1 ss into first dc.
13th Row: 1 ss into each of next 3 sts, * 1 dc into next tr, 11 ch, miss 8 sts, 1 dc into next tr, 5 ch, miss 8 sts; repeat from * ending with 1 ss into first dc.
14th Row: 1 ss into next loop, 2 ch, into same loop work 1 tr (3 ch and a 2 tr cluster) 7 times, * a 2 tr cluster into centre ch of next loop, into next loop work (a 2 tr cluster, 3 ch) 7 times and a 2 tr cluster; repeat from * ending with a 2 tr cluster into centre ch of next loop, 1 ss into first tr.
15th Row: * (Into next loop work 1 dc 3 ch and 1 dc) 7 times, 1 ss into each of next 3 sts; repeat from * all round. Fasten off.

Damp and pull into shape over jar. Thread ribbon through spaces to fit neck of jar, draw up and tie neatly in a bow.

COVER NO. 2: Commence with 7 ch, join with a ss to form a ring.
1st Row: 3 ch, 17 tr into ring, 1 ss into 3rd of 3 ch.
2nd Row: 1 dc into same place as ss, * 7 ch, miss 2 tr, 1 dc into next tr; repeat from * ending with 7 ch, 1 ss into first dc.
3rd Row: Into each loop work 1 dc 1 hlf tr 3 tr 3 ch 3 tr 1 hlf tr and 1 dc, 1 ss into first dc.
4th Row: 1 ss into each of next 4 sts and into loop, 3 ch, 1 dbl tr into same loop * (5 ch, leaving the last loop of each on hook work 2 dbl tr into same loop, thread over and draw through all loops on hook – a 2 dbl tr cluster made) 3 times, 2 ch, a 2 dbl tr cluster into next loop; repeat from * omitting a 2 dbl tr cluster at end of last repeat, 1 ss into first dbl tr.
5th Row: 1 ss into each of next 2 ch, 1 dc into same loop, * 5 ch, 1 dc into next 5 ch loop; repeat from * ending with 1 ch, 1 dbl tr into first dc.
6th Row: Into loop just formed work 1 dc 3 ch and 1 dc, * 5 ch, into next loop work 1 dc 3 ch and 1 dc; repeat from * ending with 1 ch, 1 dbl tr into first dc.
7th Row: Into loop just formed work 1 dc 3 ch and 1 dc, * 6 ch, into next 5 ch loop work 1 dc 3 ch and 1 dc; repeat from * ending with 2 ch, 1 dbl tr into first dc.
8th Row: Into loop just formed work 1 dc 3 ch and 1 dc, * 7 ch, into next 6 ch loop work 1 dc 3 ch and 1 dc; repeat from * ending with 2 ch, 1 trip tr into first dc.
9th Row: Into loop just formed work 1 dc 3 ch and 1 dc, * 7 ch, into next 7 ch loop work 1 dc 3 ch and 1 dc; repeat from * ending with 7 ch, 1 ss into first dc.
10th Row: 1 ss into next loop, 1 dc into same loop, * into next loop work 5 tr 3 ch and 5 tr, 1 dc into next loop; repeat from * omitting 1 dc at end of last repeat, 1 ss into first dc.
11th Row: 1 ss into each of next 5 tr and into next loop, 3 ch, into same loop work 1 dbl tr (5 ch and a 2 dbl tr cluster) 3 times, * 5 ch, into next loop work 1 dc 3 ch and 1 dc, 5 ch, into next loop work (a 2 dbl tr cluster, 5 ch) 3 times and a 2 dbl tr cluster; repeat from * ending with 5 ch, into next loop work 1 dc 3 ch and 1 dc, 5 ch, 1 ss into first dbl tr.
12th Row: 1 ss into each of next 2 ch, 1 dc into same loop, * 5 ch, into next loop work 1 dc 5 ch and 1 dc, 5 ch, 1 dc into next loop, 5 ch, into next 3 ch loop work 1 dc 3 ch and 1 dc, 5 ch, miss next loop, 1 dc into next loop; repeat from * omitting 1 dc at end of last repeat, 1 ss into first dc. Fasten off.

Damp and pin out to shape.
Thread ribbon through row of loops to fit neck of jar, draw up and tie neatly in a bow.

TEA

Crochet bowl

MATERIALS: Coats Chain Mercer-Crochet Cotton No. 20 (20 g): 1 ball. This model is worked in White, but any shade of Mercer-Crochet may be used. Milward steel crochet hook 1,25 mm.

TENSION: First 5 rows – 5,5 cm in diameter.

MEASUREMENTS: Depth of side – 9 cm. Top Edge – 16,5 cm in diameter.

ABBREVIATIONS: See p. 3

BASE

Commence with 9 ch, join with a ss to form a ring.

1st Row: 3 ch, 31 tr into ring, 1 ss into 3rd of 3 ch.

2nd Row: 3 ch, 1 tr into each of next 2 tr, * 2 tr into next tr, 1 tr into each of next 3 tr; repeat from * ending with 2 tr into next tr, 1 ss into 3rd of 3 ch.

3rd Row: 1 dc into same place as ss, * 2 ch, miss 1 tr, 1 dc into next tr; repeat from * ending with 2 ch, 1 ss into first dc.

4th Row: 1 ss into first loop, 3 ch, 3 tr into same loop, 4 tr into each loop, 1 ss into 3rd of 3 ch.

5th Row: 3 ch, 1 tr into each tr, 1 ss into 3rd of 3 ch.

6th Row: As 3rd row.

7th Row: 1 ss into first loop, 3 ch, 2 tr into same loop, 3 tr into each loop, 1 ss into 3rd of 3 ch.

8th Row: 1 dc into same place as ss, 1 dc into each tr, 1 ss into back loop of first dc.

SIDE:

1st Row: 1 dc into same place as ss, 1 dc into back loop of each dc, 1 ss into first dc.

2nd Row: 3 ch, 1 tr into each dc, 1 ss into 3rd of 3 ch.

3rd Row: as 5th row of base.

4th Row: 1 dc into same place as ss, * 5 ch, miss 2 tr, 1 dc into next tr; repeat from * ending with 1 ch, 1 dbl tr into first dc.

5th Row: 1 ss into loop just formed, 3 ch, 4 tr into same loop, remove loop from hook, insert hook into 3rd of 3 ch and draw dropped loop through – a starting popcorn st made, * 5 ch, 1 dc into next loop, 5 ch, 5 tr into next loop, remove loop from hook, insert hook into first tr of tr group and draw dropped loop through (a popcorn st made); repeat from * omitting a popcorn st at end of last repeat, 1 ss into first popcorn st.

6th Row: * 1 dc into next loop, 9 ch, 1 dc into next loop; repeat from * ending with 1 ss into first dc.

7th Row: 1 ss into next loop, 3 ch, a starting popcorn st into same loop, * (3 ch, a popcorn st into same loop) 4 times, 9 dc into next loop, a popcorn st into next loop; repeat from * omitting a popcorn st at end of last repeat, 1 ss into first popcorn st.

8th Row: 1 ss into next loop, 3 ch, a starting popcorn st into same loop, * (3 ch, a popcorn st into next loop) 3 times, 5 ch, miss 4 dc, 1 dc into next dc, 5 ch, a popcorn st into next loop; repeat from * omitting a popcorn st at end of last repeat, 1 ss into first popcorn st.

9th Row: 1 ss into next loop, 3 ch, a starting popcorn st into same loop, * (3 ch, a popcorn st into next loop) twice, (5 ch, 1 dc into next loop) twice, 5 ch, a popcorn st into next loop; repeat from * omitting a popcorn st at end of last repeat, 1 ss into first popcorn st.

10th Row: 1 ss into next loop, 3 ch, a starting popcorn st into same loop, * 3 ch, a popcorn st into next loop, (5 ch, 1 dc into next loop) 3 times, 5 ch, a popcorn st into next loop; repeat from * omitting a popcorn st at end of last repeat, 1 ss into first popcorn st.

11th Row: 1 ss into next loop, 3 ch, a starting popcorn st into same loop, * 5 ch, (1 tr into centre ch of next loop) twice, 11 ch, (1 tr into centre ch of next loop) twice, 5 ch, a popcorn st into next loop; repeat from * omitting a popcorn st at end of last repeat, 1 ss into first popcorn st.

12th Row: 1 dc into same place as ss, * 5 dc into next loop, into next loop work (a popcorn st, 3 ch) 5 times and a popcorn st, 5 dc into next loop, 1 dc into next popcorn st; repeat from * omitting 1 dc at end of last repeat, 1 ss into first dc.

13th Row: 1 dc into same place as ss, * 5 ch, a popcorn st into next loop, (3 ch, a popcorn st into next loop) 4 times, 5 ch, miss 5 dc, 1 dc into next dc; repeat from * omitting 5 ch and 1 dc at end of last repeat, 2 ch, 1 tr into first dc.

14th Row: 1 dc into loop just formed, * 5 ch, 1 dc into next loop, 5 ch, (a popcorn st into next loop, 3 ch) 3 times, a popcorn st into next loop, 5 ch, 1 dc into next loop; repeat from * omitting 5 ch and 1 dc at end of last repeat, 2 ch, 1 tr into first dc.

15th Row: 1 dc into loop just formed, * (5 ch, 1 dc into next loop) twice, 5 ch, (a popcorn st into next loop, 3 ch) twice, a popcorn st into next loop, 5 ch, 1 dc into next loop; repeat from * omitting 5 ch and 1 dc at end of last repeat, 2 ch, 1 tr into first dc.

16th Row: 3 ch, * 1 tr into centre ch of next loop, 9 ch, (1 tr into centre ch of next loop) twice, 5 ch, a popcorn st into next loop, 3 ch, a popcorn st into next loop, 5 ch, 1 tr into centre ch of next loop; repeat from * omitting 1 tr at end of last repeat, 1 ss into 3rd of 3 ch.

17th Row: 1 ss into next tr and into next loop, 3 ch, a starting popcorn st into same loop, * (3 ch, a popcorn st into same loop) 4 times, 3 dc into next loop, 4 ch, a popcorn st into next loop, 4 ch, 3 dc into next loop, a popcorn st into next loop; repeat from * omitting a popcorn st at end of last repeat, 1 ss into first popcorn st.

18th Row: * Into each of next 4 loops work 1 dc 3 ch and 1 dc, miss 1 dc, 1 dc into next dc, 4 dc into next loop, into next popcorn st work 1 dc 3 ch and 1 dc, 4 dc into next loop, miss 1 dc, 1 dc into next dc; repeat from * ending with 1 ss into first dc. Fasten off.

Starch firmly, pull into shape and leave to dry.

Doily

MATERIALS: Tridalia No. 8 (50 g ball). Two balls selected colour. Milward steel crochet hook 1,00 mm.

MEASUREMENTS: Finished size of doily 66 cm in diameter.

TENSION: First 7 rows of doily 4,5 cm in diameter.

ABBREVIATIONS: See p. 3

DOILY: Commence with 15 ch, join with a ss to form a ring.

1st Row: Into ring work 32 dc, 1 ss into first dc.

2nd Row: 4 ch, * miss next dc, 1 tr into next dc, 1 ch; rep from * ending with 1 ss into 3rd of 4 ch.

3rd Row: 5 ch, *1 dc into next lp, 4 ch; rep from * all round ending with 1 ss into 1st of 5 ch.

4th to 7th Row: 1 ss into each of next 2 ch, 1 dc into same lp, * 5 ch, 1 dc into next lp; rep from * omitting 1 dc at end of last rep, 1 ss into first dc.

8th Row: 1 dc into next lp, 3 ch, * 5 dbl tr into same lp, 5 ch, 1 dc into next lp, 5 ch, 1 dbl tr into next lp; rep from * omitting 1 dbl tr at end of last rep, 1 ss into 3rd of 3 ch.

9th Row: 4 ch, * 1 dbl tr into each of next 5 dbl tr, 9 ch, 1 dbl tr into next dbl tr, rep from * omitting 1 dbl tr at end of last rep, 1 ss into 4th of 4 ch.

10th Row: 1 dc into next dbl tr, 3 ch, * 1 dbl tr into each of next 3 dbl tr, 5 ch, into next lp work 1 dbl tr 2 ch and 1 dbl tr, 5 ch, miss next dbl tr, 1 dbl tr into next dbl tr; rep from * omitting 1 dbl tr at end of last rep, 1 ss into 3rd of 3 ch.

11th Row: 1 ss into next dbl tr, 4 ch, * 1 dbl tr into next dbl tr, 6 ch, miss next lp, into next lp work 1 dbl tr 4 ch and 1 dbl tr, 6 ch, miss next dbl tr, 1 dbl tr into next dbl tr; rep from * omitting 1 dbl tr at end of last rep, 1 ss into 4th of 4 ch.

12th Row: 1 ss into next dbl tr, 4 ch, * 8 ch, miss next lp, 6 dbl tr into next lp, 8 ch, miss next dbl tr, 1 dbl tr into next dbl tr; rep from * omitting 1 dbl tr at end of last rep, 1 ss into 4th of 12 ch.

13th Row: 6 ch, 1 dbl tr into same place as ss, * 8 ch, 1 dbl tr into each of next 6 dbl tr, 8 ch, into next dbl tr work 1 dbl tr 2 ch and 1 dbl tr; rep from * omitting 1 dbl tr 2 ch and 1 dbl tr at end of last rep, 1 ss into 4th of 6 ch.

14th Row: 1 ss into next lp, 4 ch, * 3 dbl tr into same lp, 9 ch, (1 dc into next db tr, 4 ch) 5 times, 1 dc into next dbl tr, 9 ch, 1 dbl tr into next dbl tr; rep from * omitting 1 dbl tr at end of last rep, 1 ss into 4th of 4 ch.

15th Row: 4 ch, * 1 dbl tr into next dbl tr, 2 ch, 1 dbl tr into each of next 2 dbl tr, 9 ch, miss next lp, (1 dc into next lp, 4 ch) 4 times, 1 dc into next lp, 9 ch, 1 dbl tr into next dbl tr; rep from * omitting 1 dbl tr at end of lst rep, 1 ss into 4th of 4 ch.

16th Row: 4 ch, *1 dbl tr into next dbl tr, 2 ch, into next lp work 1 dbl tr 4 ch and 1 dbl tr, 2 ch, 1 dbl tr into each of next 2 dbl tr, 8 ch, miss next lp, (1 dc into next lp, 4 ch) 3 times, 1 dc into next lp, 8 ch, 1 dbl tr into next dbl tr; rep from * omitting 1 dbl tr at end of last rep, 1 ss into 4th of 4 ch.

17th Row: 4 ch, * 1 dbl tr into next dbl tr, 3 ch, miss next lp, 8 dbl tr into next lp, 3 ch, miss next dbl tr, 1 dbl tr into each of next 2 dbl tr, 8 ch, miss next lp, (1 dc into next lp, 4 ch) twice, 1 dc into next lp, 8 ch, 1 dbl tr into next dbl tr; rep from * omitting 1 dbl tr at end of last rep, 1 ss into 4th of 4 ch.

18th Row: 4 ch, * 1 dbl tr into next dbl tr, 3 ch, (1 dbl tr into next dbl tr, 1 ch) 7 times, 1 dbl tr into next dbl tr, 2 ch, 1 dbl tr into each of next 2 dbl tr, 8 ch, miss next lp, 1 dc into next lp, 5 ch, 1 dc into next lp, 8 ch, 1 dbl tr into next dbl tr; rep from * omitting 1 dbl tr at end of last rep, 1 ss into 4th of 4 ch.

19th Row: 4 ch, * 1 dbl tr into next dbl tr, 4 ch, 1 dc into next dbl tr, (5 ch, 1 dc into next lp) 7 times, 4 ch, miss next dbl tr, 1 dbl tr into each of next 2 dbl tr, 8 ch, miss next lp, 1 dc into next lp, 8 ch, 1 dbl tr into next dbl tr; rep from * omitting 1 dbl tr at end of last rep, 1 ss into 4th of 4 ch.

20th Row: 4 ch, * 1 dbl tr into next dbl tr, 5 ch, miss next lp, (1 dc into next lp, 5 ch) 6 times, 1 dc into next lp, 5 ch, 1 dbl tr into each of the next 2 dbl tr, 8 ch, 1 dc into next dc, 8 ch, 1 dbl tr into next dbl tr; rep from * omitting 1 dbl tr at end of last rep, 1 ss into 4th of 4 ch.

21st Row: 4 ch, * 1 dbl tr into next dbl tr, 6 ch, miss next lp, (1 dc into next lp, 5 ch) 5 times, 1 dc into next lp, 6 ch, 1 dbl tr into each of next 2 dbl tr, 7 ch, 1 dbl tr into next dbl tr; rep from * omitting 1 dbl tr at end of last rep, 1 ss into 4th of 4 ch.

22nd Row: 4 ch, * 1 dbl tr into next dbl tr, 6 ch, miss next lp, (1 dc into next lp, 5 ch) 4 times, 1 dc into next lp, 6 ch, 1 dbl tr into each of next 2 dbl tr, 4 ch, miss next 3 ch, into next ch work 1 dbl tr 2 ch and 1 dbl tr, 4 ch, 1 dbl tr into next dbl tr; rep from * omitting 1 dbl tr at end of last rep, 1 ss into 4th of 4 ch.

23rd Row: 4 ch, * 1 dbl tr into next dbl tr, 7 ch, miss next lp, (1 dc into next lp, 5 ch) 3 times, 1 dc into next lp, 7 ch, 1 dbl tr into each of next 2 dbl tr, 4 ch, miss next lp, 4 dbl tr into next lp, 4 ch, 1 dbl tr into next dbl tr; rep from * omitting 1 dbl tr at end of last rep, 1 ss into 4th of 4 ch.

24th Row: 4 ch, * 1 dbl tr into next dbl tr, 7 ch, miss next lp, (1 dc into next lp, 5 ch) twice, 1 dc into next lp, 7 ch, (1 dbl tr into each of next 2 dbl tr, 5 ch) 3 times, 1 dbl tr into next dbl tr; rep from* omitting 1 dbl tr at end of last rep, 1 ss into 4th of 4 ch.

25th Row: 4 ch, * 1 dbl tr into next dbl tr, 7 ch, miss next lp, 1 dc into next lp, 6 ch, 1 dc into next lp, 7 ch, 1 dbl tr into each of next 2 dbl tr, 5 ch, miss next 4 ch, 1 dbl tr into next ch, 1 dbl tr into next dbl tr, 4 ch, miss next 2 ch, 1 dbl tr into next ch, 4 ch, miss next dbl tr, 1 dbl tr into next dbl tr, 1 dbl tr into next ch, 5 ch, 1 dbl tr into next dbl tr; rep from * omitting 1 dbl tr at end of last rep, 1 ss into 4th of 4 ch.

26th Row: 4 ch, * 1 dbl tr into next dbl tr, 8 ch, miss next lp, 1 dc into next lp, 8 ch, 1 dbl tr into each of next 2 dbl tr, 5 ch, miss next 4 ch, 1 dbl tr into each of next 2 sts, 5 ch, miss next dbl tr, into next dbl tr work 1 dbl tr 2 ch and 1 dbl tr, 5 ch, miss next dbl tr, 1 dbl tr into each of next 2 sts, 5 ch, 1 dbl tr into next dbl tr; rep from * omitting 1 dbl tr at end of last rep, 1 ss into 4th of 4 ch.

27th Row: 4 ch, * 1 dbl tr into next dbl tr, 7 ch, 1 dbl tr into next dc, 7 ch, 1 dbl tr into each of next 2 dbl tr, 7 ch, miss next 4 ch, 1 dbl tr into each of next 2 sts, 7 ch, miss next 4 ch, 1 dbl tr into each of next 2 sts, 7 ch, miss next dbl tr, 1 dbl tr into next dbl tr, 3 ch, 1 dbl tr into next dbl tr, 7 ch, miss next dbl tr, 1 dbl tr into each of next 2 sts, 7 ch, 1 dbl tr into next dbl tr; rep from * omitting 1 dbl tr at end of last rep, 1 ss into 4th of 4 ch.

28th Row: 1 ss into each of next 3 ch, 4 ch, * 1 dbl tr into next ch, 7 ch, miss 3 ch on next lp, 1 dbl tr into each of next 2 ch, 7 ch, 3 dbl tr into next lp, 7 ch, miss 6 ch on next lp, 1 dbl tr into next ch, 2 dbl tr into next dbl tr, 3 ch, 1 dbl tr into centre ch on next lp, 3 ch, 2 dbl tr into next dbl tr, 1 dbl tr into next ch, 7 ch, 3 dbl tr into next lp, 7 ch, miss 2 ch, 1 dbl tr into next ch; rep from * omitting 1 dbl tr at end of last rep, 1 ss into 4th of 4 ch.

29th Row: 8 ch, * miss next 3 ch, 1 dbl tr into next ch, 4 ch, miss next dbl tr, 1 dbl tr into each of next 2 sts, 6 ch, 1 dbl tr into each of next 3 dbl tr, 6 ch, miss next 6 ch, 1 dbl tr into next ch, 1 dbl tr into next dbl tr, 2 dbl tr into next dbl tr, 1 dbl tr into next dbl tr, 2 ch, into next dbl tr work 1 dbl tr 3 ch and 1 dbl tr, 2 ch, 1 dbl tr into next dbl tr, 2 dbl tr into next dbl tr, 1 dbl tr into each of next 2 sts, 6 ch, 1 dbl tr into each of next 3 dbl tr, 5 ch, miss next 6 ch, 1 dbl tr into each of next 2 sts, 4 ch; rep from * omitting 1 dbl tr and 4 ch at end of last rep, 1 ss into 4th of 8 ch.

30th Row: 1 ss into last dbl tr made, 9 ch, * into next dbl tr work 1 dbl tr 3 ch and 1 dbl tr, 5 ch, miss next dbl tr, 1 dbl tr into each of next 2 sts, 5 ch, 1 dbl tr into each of next 3 dbl tr, 6 ch, 1 dbl tr into each of next 5 dbl tr (3 ch, 1 dbl tr into next dbl tr) 3 times, 1 dbl tr into each of next 4 dbl tr, 6 ch, 1 dbl tr into each of next 3 dbl tr, 5 ch, miss next 4 ch, 1 dbl tr into each of next 2 sts, 5 ch, miss next dbl tr; rep from * omitting 1 dbl tr and 5 ch at end of last rep, 1 ss into 4th of 9 ch.

31st Row: 1 ss into last dbl tr made, 9 ch, * miss next dbl tr, (1 dbl tr into next dbl tr, 5 ch) twice, miss next dbl tr, 1 dbl tr into each of next 2 sts, 5 ch, ** 1 dbl tr into each of next 3 dbl tr, 6 ch, miss next dbl tr, 1 dbl tr into each of next 3 dbl tr, 3 ch, miss next 2 ch, 1 dbl tr into next ch, 2 dbl tr into next dbl tr, 3 ch, miss next ch, 1 dbl tr into next ch, 3 ch, 2 dbl tr into next dbl tr, 1 dbl tr into next ch, 3 ch, miss next dbl tr, 1 dbl tr into each of next 3 dbl tr, 6 ch, 1 dbl tr into each of next 3 dbl tr **, 5 ch, miss next 4 ch, 1 dbl tr into each of next 2 sts, 5 ch; rep from * omitting 1 dbl tr and 5 ch at end of last rep, 1 ss into 4th of 9 ch.

32nd Row: 1 ss into each of next 5 ch, 4 ch, * 2 dbl tr into next dbl tr, 3 ch, 1 dbl tr into centre ch on next lp, 3 ch, 2 dbl tr into next dbl tr, 1 dbl tr into next ch, 7 ch, miss next 2 dbl tr, 1 dbl tr into each of next 3 dbl tr, 7 ch, ** miss next dbl tr, 1 dbl tr into next dbl tr, 3 ch, miss next 2 ch, 1 dbl tr into next ch, 1 dbl tr into next dbl tr, 2 dbl tr into next dbl tr, 1 dbl tr into next dbl tr, 3 ch, into next dbl tr work 1 dbl tr 3 ch and 1 dbl tr, 3 ch, 1 dbl tr into next dbl tr, 2 dbl tr into next dbl tr, 1 dbl tr into each of next 2 sts, 3 ch, miss next dbl tr, 1 dbl tr into next dbl tr **, 7 ch, 1 dbl tr into each of next 3 dbl tr, 7 ch, miss next 2 dbl tr and 4 ch on next lp, 1 dbl tr into next ch; rep from * omitting 1 dbl tr at end of last rep, 1 ss into 4th of 4 ch.

33rd Row: 4 ch, * 2 dbl tr into next dbl tr, 1 dbl tr into next dbl tr, 3 ch, into next dbl tr work 1 dbl tr 3 ch and 1 dbl tr, 3 ch, 1 dbl tr into next dbl tr, 2 dbl tr into next dbl tr, 1 dbl tr into each of next 2 sts, 6 ch, ** 1 dbl tr into each of next 3 dbl tr, 7 ch, miss next dbl tr, 1 dbl tr into each of next 5 dbl tr, 3 ch, 1 dbl tr into next dbl tr, 4 ch, 1 dbl tr into next dbl tr, 3 ch, 1 dbl tr into each of next 5 dbl tr, 7 ch, miss next dbl tr, 1 dbl tr into each of next 3 dbl tr **, 6 ch, miss next 6 ch, 1 dbl tr into each of next 2 sts; rep from * omitting 1 dbl tr at end of last rep, 1 ss into 4th of 4 ch.

34th Row: 4 ch, * 1 dbl tr into each of next 3 dbl tr, 3 ch, 1 dbl tr into next dbl tr, 5 ch, 1 dbl tr into next dbl tr, 3 ch, 1 dbl tr into each of next 5 dbl tr, 5 ch, rep from ** to ** on 31st row, 5 ch, 1 dbl tr into each of next 2 dbl tr; rep from * omitting 1 dbl tr at end of last rep, 1 ss into 4th of 4 ch

35th Row: 4 ch, * 1 dbl tr into each of next 2 dbl tr, 3 ch, miss next 2 ch, 1 dbl tr into next ch, 2 dbl tr into next dbl tr, 3 ch, miss next 2 ch, 1 dbl tr into next ch, 3 ch, 2 dbl tr into next dbl tr, 1 dbl tr into next ch, 3 ch, miss next dbl tr, 1 dbl tr into each of next 3 dbl tr, 5 ch, 1 dbl tr into each of next 3 dbl tr, 6 ch, rep from ** to ** on 32nd row, 6 ch, 1 dbl tr into each of next 3 dbl tr, 5 ch, miss next dbl tr, 1 dbl tr into next dbl tr; rep from * omitting 1 dbl tr at end of last rep, 1 ss into 4th of 4 ch.

36th Row: 1 ss into next dbl tr, 7 ch, * miss next 2 ch, 1 dbl tr into each of next 2 sts, 2 dbl tr into next dbl tr, 1 dbl tr into next dbl tr, 3 ch, into next dbl tr work 1 dbl tr 3 ch and 1 dbl tr, 3 ch, 1 dbl tr into next dbl tr, 2 dbl tr into next dbl tr, 1 dbl tr into each of next 2 sts, 3 ch, miss next dbl tr, 1 dbl tr into next dbl tr **, 5 ch, rep from ** to ** on 33rd row, 5 ch, miss next dbl tr, 1 dbl tr into next dbl tr, 3 ch; rep from* omitting 1 dbl tr and 3 ch at end of last rep, 1 ss into 4th of 7 ch.

37th Row: 1 ss into each of next 4 sts, 4 ch, * 1 dbl tr into each of next 4 dbl tr, 3 ch, 1 dbl tr into next dbl tr, 4 ch, 1 dbl tr into next dbl tr, 3 ch, 1 dbl tr into each of next 5 dbl tr, 7 ch, miss next dbl tr, rep from ** to ** on 31 st row working 7 ch instead of 6,7 ch, miss next dbl tr, 1 dbl tr into next dbl tr; rep from * omitting 1 dbl tr at end of last rep, 1 ss into 4th of 4 ch.

38th Row: 1 ss into next dbl tr, 4 ch, * 1 dbl tr into each of next 2 dbl tr, 3 ch, miss next 2 ch, ** 1 dbl tr into next ch, 2 dbl tr into next dbl tr, 3 ch, miss next ch, 1 dbl tr into next ch, 3 ch, 2 dbl tr into next dbl tr, 1 dbl tr into next ch, 3 ch **, (miss next dbl tr, 1 dbl tr into each of next 3 dbl tr, 7 ch) twice, rep from ** to ** on 32nd row, 7 ch, 1 dbl tr into each of next 3 dbl tr, 7 ch, miss next dbl tr, 1 dbl tr into next dbl tr; rep from * omitting 1 dbl tr at end of last rep. 1 ss into 4th of 4 ch.

39th Row: 1 ss into next dbl tr, 7 ch, * rep from * to ** on 36th row, 7 ch, miss next dbl tr, 1 dbl tr into each of next 3 dbl tr, 7 ch, miss next dbl tr, 1 dbl tr into each of next 5 dbl tr, (4 ch, 1 dbl tr into next dbl tr) 3 times, 1 dbl tr into each of next 4 dbl tr, 7 ch, miss next dbl tr, 1 dbl tr into each of next 3 dbl tr, 7 ch, miss next dbl tr, 1 dbl tr into next dbl tr; rep from first * on this row omitting 1 dbl tr at end of last rep, 1 ss into 4th of 7 ch.

40th Row: 1 ss into each of next 4 sts, 4 ch, * 1 dbl tr into each of next 4 dbl tr, (4 ch, 1 dbl tr into next dbl tr) 3 times, 1 dbl tr into each of next 4 dbl tr, ** (7 ch, miss next dbl tr, 1 dbl tr into each of next 3 dbl tr) twice, 4 ch, miss next 3 ch, 1 dbl tr into next ch, 2 dbl tr into next dbl tr, 3 ch, miss next ch, 1 dbl tr into next ch, 3 ch, 2 dbl tr into next dbl tr, 1 dbl tr into next ch, 4 ch, (miss next dbl tr, 1 dbl tr into each of next 3 dbl tr, 7 ch) twice **, miss next dbl tr, 1 dbl tr into next dbl tr; rep from * omitting 1 dbl tr at end of last rep, 1 ss into 4th of 4 ch.

41st Row: 1 ss into next dbl tr, 4 ch, * 1

dbl tr into each of next 2 dbl tr, 4 ch, miss next 3 ch, rep from ** to ** on 38th row, (miss next dbl tr, 1 dbl tr into each of next 3 dbl tr, 8 ch) twice, miss next dbl tr, 1 dbl tr into next dbl tr, 4 ch, miss next 3 ch, 1 dbl tr into each of next 2 sts, 2 dbl tr into next dbl tr, 1 dbl tr into next dbl tr, 3 ch, into next dbl tr work 1 dbl tr 3 ch and 1 dbl tr, 3 ch, 1 dbl tr into next dbl tr, 2 dbl tr into next dbl tr, 1 dbl tr into each of next 2 sts, 4 ch, miss next dbl tr, 1 dbl tr into next dbl tr, 8 ch, miss next dbl tr, 1 dbl tr into each of next 3 dbl tr, 8 ch, miss next dbl tr, 1 dbl tr into next dbl tr; rep from * omitting 1 dbl tr at end of last rep, 1 ss into 4th of 4 ch.

42nd Row: 1 ss into next dbl tr, 8 ch, * miss next 3 ch, 1 dbl tr into each of next 2 sts, 2 dbl tr into next dbl tr, 1 dbl tr into next dbl tr, 4 ch, into next dbl tr work 1 dbl tr 3 ch and 1 dbl tr, 4 ch, 1 dbl tr into next dbl tr, 2 dbl tr into next dbl tr, 1 dbl tr into each of next 2 sts, 4 ch, miss next dbl tr, 1 dbl tr into next dbl tr, 9 ch, miss next dbl tr, 1 dbl tr into each of next 3 dbl tr, ** 9 ch, miss next dbl tr, 1 dbl tr into each of next 5 dbl tr, (4 ch, 1 dbl tr into next dbl tr) 3 times, 1 dbl tr into each of next 4 dbl tr, 9 ch, miss next dbl tr, 1 dbl tr into each of next 3 dbl tr, **, 9 ch, miss next dbl tr, 1 dbl tr into next dbl tr, 4 ch; rep from * omitting 1 dbl tr and 4 ch at end of last rep, 1 ss into 4th of 8 ch.

43rd Row: 1 ss into each of next 5 sts, 4 ch, * 1 dbl tr into each of next 4 dbl tr, (4 ch, 1 dbl tr into next dbl tr) 3 times, 1 dbl tr into each of next 4 dbl tr, rep from ** to ** on 40th row working 9 ch instead of 7, miss next dbl tr, 1 dbl tr into next dbl tr; rep from * omitting 1 dbl tr at end of last rep, 1 ss into 4th of 4 ch.

44th Row: As 41st row always working 9 ch instead of 8 ch.

45th Row: 1 ss into next dbl tr, 8 ch, * miss next 3 ch, 1 dbl tr into each of next 2 sts, 2 dbl tr into next dbl tr, 1 dbl tr into next dbl tr, 3 ch, into next dbl tr work 1 dbl tr 3 ch and 1 dbl tr, 3 ch, 1 dbl tr into next dbl tr, 2 dbl tr into next dbl tr, 1 dbl tr into each of next 2 sts, 4 ch, miss next dbl tr, 1 dbl tr into next dbl tr, 8 ch, miss next dbl tr, 1 dbl tr into each of next 3 dbl tr, rep from ** to ** on 42nd row, 8 ch, miss next dbl tr, 1 dbl tr into next dbl tr, 4 ch; rep from * omitting 1 dbl tr and 4 ch at end of last rep, 1 ss into 4th of 8 ch.

46th Row: As 43rd row always working 10 ch instead of 7 ch.

47th Row: As 41st row always working 10 ch instead of 8 ch.

48th Row: As 45th row always working 12 ch instead of 9 ch.

49th Row: 1 ss into each of next 5 sts, 4 ch, * 1 dbl tr into each of next 4 dbl tr, 7 ch, miss next lp, 3 dbl tr into next lp, 7 ch, miss next dbl tr, 1 dbl tr into each of next 5 dbl tr, 8 ch, miss next lp, 8 dbl tr into next lp, 1 dbl tr into each of next 3 dbl tr, 8 dbl tr into next lp, 7 ch, miss next dbl tr, 1 dbl tr into each of next 3 dbl tr, 7 ch, miss next lp, 3 dbl tr into next lp, 7 ch, miss next 2 dbl tr, 1 dbl tr into each of next 3 dbl tr, 7 ch, 8 dbl tr into next lp, 1 dbl tr into each of next 3 dbl tr, 8 dbl tr into next lp, 8 ch, miss next dbl tr, 1 dbl tr into next dbl tr; rep from * omitting 1 dbl tr at end of last rep, 1 ss into 4th of 4 ch.

50th Row: 1 ss into next dbl tr, 4 ch, * 1 dbl tr into each of next 2 dbl tr, 6 ch, miss next 6 ch, 1 dbl tr into each of next 5 sts, 6 ch, miss next dbl tr, 1 dbl tr into each of next 3 dbl tr, 6 ch, 2 dbl tr into next lp, 1 dbl tr into each of next 4 dbl tr, 5 ch, miss next 3 dbl tr, 1 dbl tr into each of next 5 dbl tr, 5 ch, miss next 3 dbl tr, 1 dbl tr into each of next 4 dbl tr, 2 dbl tr into next lp, 6 ch, miss next dbl tr, 1 dbl tr into next dbl tr, 6 ch, miss next 6 ch, 1 dbl tr into each of next 5 sts, 6 ch, miss next dbl tr, 1 dbl tr into next dbl tr, 6 ch, 2 dbl tr into next lp, 1 dbl tr into each of next 4 dbl tr, 5 ch, miss next 3 dbl tr, 1 dbl tr into each of next 5 dbl tr, 5 ch, miss next 3 dbl tr, 1 dbl tr into each of next 4 dbl tr, 2 dbl tr into next lp, 6 ch, miss next dbl tr, 1 dbl tr into next dbl tr; rep from * omitting 1 dbl tr at end of last rep, 1 ss into 4th of 4 ch.

51st Row: 1 ss into next dbl tr, 10 ch, * miss next dbl tr, 1 dbl tr into each of next 5 dbl tr, 6 ch, miss next dbl tr, 1 dbl tr into next dbl tr, 5 ch, ** 3 dbl tr into next lp, 1 dbl tr into each of next 4 dbl tr, 6 ch, miss next 2 dbl tr, 1 dbl tr into each of next 3 dbl tr, 1 ch, 1 dbl tr into same place as last dbl tr, 1 dbl tr into each of next 2 dbl tr, 6 ch, miss next 2 dbl tr, 1 dbl tr into each of next 4 dbl tr, 3 dbl tr into next lp **, 9 ch, miss next dbl tr, 1 dbl tr into each of next 5 dbl tr, 9 ch, miss next dbl tr, rep from ** to ** on this row, 6 ch, miss next dbl tr, 1 dbl tr into next dbl tr, 6 ch; rep from * omitting 1 dbl tr and 6 ch at end of last rep, 1 ss into 4th of 10 ch.

52nd Row: 1 ss into each of next 8 sts, 4 ch, * 1 dbl tr into each of next 2 dbl tr, 9 ch, miss next lp, ** 3 dbl tr into next lp, 1 dbl tr into each of next 4 dbl tr, 7 ch, miss next 3 dbl tr, 1 dbl tr into each of next 2 dbl tr, 3 ch, into next ch work, 1 dbl tr 3 ch and 1 dbl tr, 3 ch, miss next dbl tr, 1 dbl tr into each of next 2 dbl tr, 7 ch, miss next 3 dbl tr, 1 dbl tr into each of next 4 dbl tr, 3 dbl tr into next lp, 9 ch **, miss next dbl tr, 1 dbl tr into each of next 3 dbl tr, 9 ch, rep from ** to ** on this row, miss next 2 dbl tr, 1 dbl tr into next dbl tr; rep from * omitting 1 dbl tr at end of last rep, 1 ss into 4th of 4 ch.

53rd Row: 1 ss into next dbl tr, 12 ch, * 3 dbl tr into next lp, 1 dbl tr into each of next 4 dbl tr, 8 ch, miss next 3 dbl tr, 1 dbl tr into each of next 2 dbl tr, 3 ch, miss next lp, 8 dbl tr into next lp, 3 ch, miss next dbl tr, 1 dbl tr into each of next 2 dbl tr, 8 ch, miss next 3 dbl tr, 1 dbl tr into each of next 4 dbl tr, 3 dbl tr into next lp, 8 ch, miss next dbl tr, 1 dbl tr into next dbl tr, 8 ch; rep from * omitting 1 dbl tr and 8 ch at end of last rep, 1 ss into 4th of 12 ch.

54th Row: 1 ss into each of 5 ch, 4 ch, * 2 dbl tr into same lp, 1 dbl tr into each of next 4 dbl tr, 11 ch, miss next 3 dbl tr, 1 dbl tr into each of next 2 dbl tr, 4 ch, (1 dbl tr into next dbl tr, 1 ch) 7 times, 1 dbl tr into next dbl tr, 4 ch, 1 dbl tr into each of next 2 dbl tr, 11 ch, miss next 3 dbl tr, 1 dbl tr into each of next 4 dbl tr, 3 dbl tr into next lp, 10 ch, 1 dbl tr into next lp; rep from * omitting 1 dbl tr at end of last rep, 1 ss into 4th of 4 ch. Fasten off.

55th Row: Join thread to first dbl tr of any 2 dbl tr group, 1 ss into same place as join, 4 ch, * 1 dbl tr into next dbl tr, 4 ch, (1 dbl tr into next dbl tr, 2 ch) 7 times, 1 dbl tr into next dbl tr, 4 ch, 1 dbl tr into each of next 2 dbl tr, 11 ch, miss next 3 dbl tr, 1 dbl tr into each of next 4 dbl tr, 10 dbl tr into next lp, 1 dbl tr into each of next 4 dbl tr, 11 ch, 1 dbl tr into next dbl tr; rep from * omitting 1 dbl tr at end of last rep, 1 ss into 4th of 4 ch.

56th Row: 4 ch, * 1 dbl tr into next dbl tr, 5 ch, (1 dbl tr into next dbl tr, 3 ch) 7 times, 1 dbl tr into next dbl tr, 5 ch, 1 dbl tr into each of next 2 dbl tr, 13 ch, miss next 2 dbl tr, 1 dbl tr into each of next 14 dbl tr, 13 ch, miss next dbl tr, 1 dbl tr into next dbl tr; rep from * omitting 1 dbl tr at end of last rep, 1 ss into 4th of 4 ch.

57th Row: 4 ch, * 1 dbl tr into next dbl tr, 5 ch, (1 dbl tr into next dbl tr, 4 ch) 7 times, 1 dbl tr into next dbl tr, 5 ch, 1 dbl tr into each of next 2 dbl tr, 13 ch, miss next 2 dbl tr, 1 dbl tr into each of next 10 dbl tr, 13 ch, miss next 2 dbl tr, 1 dbl tr into next dbl tr; rep from * omitting 1 dbl tr at end of last rep, 1 ss into 4th of 4 ch.

58th Row: 4 ch, * 1 dbl tr into next dbl tr, 5 ch, miss next lp, (leaving the last lp of each on hook work 3 dbl tr into next lp, thread over and draw through all lps on hook – a 3 dbl tr cl made, 5 ch) 7 times, miss next dbl tr, 1 dbl tr into each of next 2 dbl tr, 13 ch, miss next 2 dbl tr, 1 dbl tr into each of next 6 dbl tr, 13 ch, miss next 2 dbl tr, 1 dbl tr into next dbl tr; rep from * omitting 1 dbl tr at end of last rep, 1 ss into 4th of 4 ch.

59th Row: 4 ch, * 1 dbl tr into next dbl tr, 7 ch, miss next lp, (a 3 dbl tr cl into next lp, 7 ch) 6 times, 1 dbl tr into each of next 2 dbl tr, 13 ch, miss next 2 dbl tr, 1 dbl tr into each of next 3 dbl tr, 13 ch, miss next dbl tr, 1 dbl tr into next dbl tr; rep from * omitting 1 dbl tr at end of last rep, 1 ss into 4th of 4 ch.

60th Row: 1 dc into same place as ss, * 1 dc into next dbl tr, into each of next 7 lps work 4 dc 3 ch and 5 dc, miss next dbl tr, 1 dc into next dbl tr, into next lp work 4 dc 3 ch 9 dc 3 ch and 4 dc, 1 dc into each of next 3 dbl tr, into next lp work 4 dc 3 ch 9 dc 3 ch and 4 dc, miss next dbl tr; rep from * ending with 1 ss into first dc. Fasten off.

Damp and pin out to measurements.

Tablecloth

MATERIALS: Tridalia No. 5 (50 g Ball): 6 balls selected colour. Milward Disc (aluminium) crochet hook 2,50 mm. A linen tablecoth 240 × 150 cm.

TENSION: 5 sps and 4 rows to 2,5 cm square.

MEASUREMENTS: Size of crochet strip 34,5 × 106,5 cm.

ABBREVIATIONS: See p. 3

TABLECLOTH: Commence with 194 ch.

1st Row: 1 tr into 8th ch from hook, (2 ch, miss next 2 ch, 1 tr into next ch) 62 times (63 sps made), 5 ch, turn.

2nd Row: Miss first tr, 1 tr into next tr (sp made over sp at beg of row), 2 tr into next lp, 1 tr into next tr, 61 times (61 blks made over 61 sps), 2 ch, miss next 2 ch, 1 tr into next ch (sp made over sp at end of row), 5 ch, turn.

3rd Row: 1 sp, 1 tr into next 3 tr (blk made over blk), (2 ch, miss next 2 tr, 1 tr into next tr) 59 times (59 sps made over 59 blks), 1 blk, 1 sp, 5 ch, turn.

4th Row: 1 sp, 1 blk, 2 ch, 1 tr into next tr (sp made over sp) and cont to follow diagram to top, then work from 62nd row to 1st row once more. Fasten off.

Centre crochet strip on tablecloth and sew in position. Cut fabric under crochet.

DIAGRAM

Three Doilies

MATERIALS: Tridalia No. 8 (50 g ball): 1 ball selected colour. Milward steel crochet hook 1,00 mm.

MEASUREMENTS: Large doily 24 cm in diameter. Small doily 16,5 cm in diameter.

TENSION: First 4 rows on small doily to 4 cm in diameter.

ABBREVIATIONS: See p. 3

SMALL DOILY (make 2): Commence with 12 ch join with a ss to form a ring.

1st Row: 3 ch, into ring work 23 tr, 1 ss into 3rd of 3 ch.

2nd Row: 3 ch, leaving the last lp of each on hook work 1 dbl tr into each of next 2 tr, thread over and draw through all lps on hook (a starting cl made), * 5 ch, a 3 dbl tr cl over next 3 tr; rep from * all round, 5 ch, 1 ss into first cl.

3rd Row: Into each lp work 9 dc, 1 ss into first dc.

4th Row: 1 ss into next dc, * 1 dc into each on next 7 dc, 13 ch, 1 tr into 8th ch from hook, 1 tr into each of next 5 ch, miss next 2 dc; rep from * ending with 1 ss into first dc.

5th Row: 1 ss into each of next 3 dc, 1 dc into same place as last ss, * 6 ch, 1 dc at base of 5th tr , 3 ch, into next 7 ch lp work 14 tr, 3 ch, miss next 2 tr, 1 dc into next tr, 6 ch, miss next 3 dc, 1 dc into next dc; rep from * omitting 1 dc at end of last rep, 1 ss into first dc.

6th Row: 1 ss into each of next 6 ch, 1 dc into next 3 ch lp, 4 ch, * (1 tr into next tr, 1 ch) 3 times, 4 ch, 1 ss into 4th ch from hook (a p made), (into each of

next 4 tr work 1 tr and 1 ch, a p) twice, 1 tr into each of next 3 tr, miss next 2 lps, into next lp work 1 tr, 1 ch; rep from * omitting 1 tr and 1 ch at end of last rep, 1 ss into 3rd of 4 ch.

7th Row: Ss to within next p, 1 dc into same place as last ss, * 7 ch, 1 dc into next p; rep from * omitting 1 dc at end of last rep, 1 ss into first dc.

8th Row: Into each lp work 9 dc, 1 ss into first dc.

9th Row: 1 ss into each of next 3 dc, * 1 dc into next dc, 8 ch, miss next 8 dc; rep from * ending with 1 ss into first dc.

10th Row: 1 ss into each of next 4 ch, 1 dc into same place as last ss, * 9 ch, 1 dc into next lp; rep from * ending with 1 ss into first dc.

11th Row: As 10th row.

12th Row: 3 ch, leaving the last lp of each on hook work 2 dbl tr into same place as ss, thread over and draw through all lps on hook (a starting cl made), * 9 ch, a 3 dbl tr cl into same place as last cl, 1 dc into next lp, 9 ch, 1 dc into next lp, a 3 dbl tr cl into next dc; rep from * omitting a cl at end of last rep, 1 ss into first cl.

13th Row: As 10th row.

14th Row: Ss to centre of next lp, 1 dc into same place as last ss, * into next dc work a 3 dbl tr cl 9 ch and a 3 dbl tr cl, 1 dc into next lp, 9 ch, 1 dc into next lp; rep from * omitting 1 dc at end of last rep, 1 ss into first dc.

15th Row: Ss to centre of next lp, 1 dc into same place as last ss, * 12 ch, 1 dc into next lp; rep from * omitting 1 dc at end of last rep, 1 ss into first dc.

16th Row: Into each lp work 8 dc a p and 8 dc, 1 ss into first dc. Fasten off.

LARGE DOILY: Commence with 16 ch, join with a ss to form a ring.

1st Row: 3 ch, into ring work 29 tr, 1 ss into 3rd of 3 ch.

2nd Row: As 2nd row of Small Doily.

Work as Small Doily from 3rd to 5th row.

6th Row: 1 ss into each of next 6 ch, 1 dc into next 3 ch lp, 4 ch, * (1 tr into next tr, 1 ch) twice, a p (into each of next 3 tr work 1 tr and 1 ch, a p) 3 times, (1 tr into next tr, 1 ch) 3 times, 1 tr into next 3 ch lp, 1 ch; rep from * omitting 1 tr and 1 ch at end of last rep, 1 ss into 3rd of 4 ch.

7th Row: As 7th row of Small Doily working 5 ch instead of 7.

8th Row: Ss to centre of next lp, 1 dc into same lp, * 5 ch, 1 dc into next lp; rep from * omitting 1 dc at end of last rep, 1 ss into first dc.

9th Row: Into each lp work 5 dc, 1 ss into first dc.

10th Row: 1 ss into each of next 2 dc, 1 dc into same place as last ss, * 7 ch, 1 dc into central dc into next lp; rep from * omitting 1 dc at end of last rep, 1 ss into first dc.

11th Row: Ss to central ch, of next lp, 1 dc into same place as last ss, * 7 ch, 1 dc into next lp; rep from * omitting 1 dc at end of last rep, 1 ss into first dc.

12th Row: A starting cl, * 5 ch, a 3 dbl tr cl into same place as last cl, 1 dc into next lp, 5 ch, 1 dc into next lp, a 3 dbl tr cl into next dc; rep from * all round omitting a cl at end of last rep, 1 ss into first cl.

13th Row: As 11th row.

14th Row: As 12th row working 7 ch instead of 5 only between cls.

15th Row: As 11th row working 9 ch instead of 7.

16th Row: As 12th row working 7 ch instead of 5 (always).

17th Row: As 15th row.

18th Row: As 12th row working 9 ch instead of 7 (always).

19th Row: As 15th row.

20th Row: As 12th row working 11 ch instead of 9 (always).

21st and 22nd Row: As 15th row working 11 ch instead of 9.

23rd Row: Into each lp work 8 dc a p and 8 dc, 1 ss into first dc. Fasten off.

Damp and pin out to measurements.

Doily

MATERIALS: Tridalia No. 8 (50 g ball): 1 ball selected colour. Milward steel crochet hook 1,00 mm.

TENSION: Size of one flower 8 cm from point to point.

MEASUREMENTS: Finished size of doily 24,5 cm in diameter.

ABBREVIATIONS: See p. 3

FIRST FLOWER: Commence with 7 ch, join with 1 ss to form a ring.
1st Row: 4 ch, leaving the last lp of each on hook work 1 tr tr into ring, thread over and draw through all lps on hook, (4 ch, leaving the last lp of each on hook work 2 tr tr into ring, thread over and draw through all lps on hook) 5 times, 4 ch, 1 ss into 1st cl. Fasten off.
2nd Row: Commence with 12 ch, join with 1 ss into top of first cl, * 1 dc into each of next 2 ch, 1 hlf tr into each of next 2 ch, 1 tr into each of next 4 ch, 1 hlf tr into each of next 2 ch, 1 dc into next ch, 3 dc into next st, working on

opposite side of ch: 1 dc into next ch, 1 hlf tr into each of next 2 ch, 1 tr into each of next 4 ch, 1 hlf tr into each of next 2 ch, 1 dc into each of next 2 ch, into next lp work 3 dc 3 ch and 3 dc. Fasten off Commence with 12 ch, 1 ss into top of next cl; rep from * all round omitting 12 ch and 1 ss at end of last rep, don't fasten off.

3rd Row: Inserting hook into back lp only work 1 ss into first dc, * 1 dc into each of next 11 dc, 3 dc into next st, 1 dc into each of next 11 dc, 5 ch, 1 ss into 3rd ch from hook, 2 ch, miss 1 dc on next petal; rep from * ending with 1 ss into first dc.

4th Row: Inserting hook into back lp only work 1 ss into next st, * 1 dc into each of next 11 dc, 3 dc into next st, 1 dc into each of next 11 dc, 3 ch, miss 1 dc on next petal; rep from * ending with 1 ss into first dc. Fasten off.

Work 9 more flowers joining each other during last row as shown on diagram with a ss at top of petals.

1st Row: With right side of flowers facing join thread to top of any petal, 1 dc into same place as join, 18 ch, 1 dc into top of next petal or joining; rep from * omitting 1 dc at end of last rep, 1 ss into first dc.

2nd Row: 1 ss into next lp, into each lp work 25 dc, 1 ss into first dc.

3rd Row: 1 dc into same place as ss, * 10 ch, miss next 11 dc, 1 dc into next dc; rep from * omitting 1 dc at end of last rep, 1 ss into first dc.

4th Row: 1 ss into next lp, into each lp work 13 dc, 1 ss into first dc.

5th Row: 1 ss into each of next 6 sts, 1 dc into same place as ss, * 10 ch, miss next 12 dc, 1 dc into next dc; rep from * omitting 1 dc at end of last rep, 1 ss into first dc.

6th Row: Work as 4th row.

7th Row: 9 ch, * miss next 6 dc, 1 tr into next dc, 4 ch, miss next 5 dc, 1 tr tr between next 2 dc, 4 ch; rep from * omitting 1 tr tr and 4 ch at end of last rep, 1 ss into 5th of 9 ch.

8th Row: 7 ch, * 1 tr into next tr, 4 ch, 1 tr into next tr tr, 4 ch; rep from * omitting 1 tr and 4 ch at end of last rep, 1 ss into 3rd of 7 ch.

9th Row: 5 ch, 1 ss into last tr on previous row, 14 tr tr into next lp to the left, 15 tr tr into each lp, 1 ss into 5th of 5 ch.

10th Row: 1 dc into tr on 8th row, 13 ch, * 1 tr into central tr tr on next group, 8 ch, 1 tr tr into next tr on 8th row, 8 ch; rep from * omitting 1 tr tr and 8 ch at end of last rep, 1 ss into 5th of 13 ch.

11th Row: 1 dc into same place as ss, * 8 ch, 1 dc into next tr, 8 ch, 1 dc into next tr tr; rep from * omitting 1 dc at end of last rep, 1 ss into first dc.

12th Row: Into each lp work 1 dc 1 hlf tr 1 tr 1 dbl tr 5 tr tr 1 dbl tr 1 tr 1 hlf tr and 1 dc.

13th Row: 1 ss into each of next 4 sts, * 1 dc into each of next 5 tr tr, 4 ch; rep from * ending with 1 ss into first dc.

14th Row: * 1 dc into each of next 3 dc, into next lp work 1 hlf tr 1 tr 7 tr tr 1 tr and 1 hlf tr, miss next dc; rep from * ending with 1 ss into first dc.

15th Row: 11 ch, * 1 tr into 4th of 7 tr tr, 6 ch, 1 tr tr into 2nd of 3 dc, 6 ch; rep from * omitting 1 tr tr and 6 ch at end of last rep, 1 ss into 5th of 11 ch.

16th Row: 1 dc into same place as ss, * 13 ch, 1 dc into next tr tr; rep from * omitting 1 dc at end of last rep, 1 ss into first dc.

17th Row: Into each lp work 21 dc.

18th and 20th Row: 1 ss into each of next 11 dc, 1 dc into same place as last ss, * 13 ch, 1 dc into central dc on next lp; rep from * omitting 1 dc at end of last rep, 1 ss into first dc.

19th and 21st Row: Work as 17th row. Fasten off.

Damp and pin out to measurements.